PRAISE FOR G

From Millennials to Gen Xers to Boomers, we're much more alike than we are different. Generation Us *gets to the heart of our shared life goals, proposing new ways we can work hand in hand to achieve social connectivity, a deep sense of community and richer lives all around. One of our missions at Silvernest is to open the door to new multi-generational housing solutions nationwide, with the aim of filling at least one piece of the larger bridge-building endeavor that* Generation Us *extols so well.*

WENDI BURKHARDT, BOOMER
CEO & Co-Founder, *Silvernest, Inc.*

—

Every organization should run to purchase Tom Matt's inspirational book Generation Us! *Working with multiple generations in our organization, Tom opens your eyes on how we all can work together for one powerful mission. Tom has an abundance of energy, has a growth mindset like no other– but what comes out loud and clear in* Generation Us *is Tom's passion and compassion for people! Keep spreading your fire– the world needs more of Tom Matt!*

CHRIS JOHNSON, BOOMER
CEO & Founder, *On Target Living*

—

I can't help but be energized and inspired by Generation Us, *and Tom Matt and his constant drive to bring the generations together. Each generation should be motivated by a common goal of growth and living the best life we can, which should instill a desire to learn from other generations as we all share our collective wisdom and experiences with each other. It's an exciting time and I am grateful to Tom for his effort in uniting, and IGNITING all of us!*

KATIE LYNWOOD, MILLENNIAL/GEN Y
Probate/Elder Law Attorney, *Buhl, Little, Lynwood & Harris, PLC*

—

PRAISE FOR *GENERATION US*

Generation Us *couldn't have come at a better time! Now, more than ever, we need to work together to bridge this 'generational gap' that has been growing over the years– especially with the direction that our nation is going. Both the older and younger generations have a lot to learn from each other, and if I can speak for the younger generation, we rely on our elders to impart wisdom on us so that we may be able to do the same one day. I had the opportunity to meet Tom Matt after a Spartan basketball game. He began asking me about school and my plans after graduation, and I shared with him that I had created a startup app and was working to scale it. It turns out that we are both working towards bridging this 'generational gap' in our own way, and that makes it easy for us to understand each other.*

MATTHEW ELEWEKE, MILLENNIAL
CEO & Founder, *Sympl.*

——

Need a jumpstart? Have you (like so many of us) found yourself a bit side-tracked on life's journey? There is no better vehicle for delivering this inspirational jolt than Tom Matt's Generation Us*! The lessons to be learned from generational sharing, support and cooperation were never more timely or relevant. Tom's message is riveted in authenticity. Don't just get a copy. Devour it. Live it. Share it. With Tom's guidance, let's demolish artificial barriers and provide cross-generational opportunities. Now that's something that'll truly benefit us all!*

JO-ANNE LEMA, BOOMER
Founder, *AfterFiftyLiving.com*

——

GENERATION US

LIVING, LOVING, LEARNING: BUILDING BENEVOLENT TOGETHERNESS

Thomas F. Matt

WITH ESSAYS AND OTHER CONTRIBUTIONS BY:

Debbie Heiser, Samantha Medved, Deb Feltz, Dave Hornak, Debbie Jamieson, Colin Milner, Bill Kost, Colin Jackson, Lisa Cini, Sky Bergman, Brandon Townsend, Mike Secord & Nick Tijerina

---

This is an anthology. The individuals contributing to the text and artwork herein have all given permission for its use.

PUBLISHED BY
Boomers Rock Media, LLC
2231 Beechnut Trail
Holt, Michigan 48842
www.boomersrock.us

FIRST PUBLICATION DATE
July 2018

---

eBook Design by Mickey Hadick
Cover Design & Custom Artwork by Miranda Miller
Book Design & Layout by Miranda Miller
Editing & Proofreading by Sandra Matt & Miranda Miller

DISCLAIMER
The material in this book concerning health-related issues should not be undertaken without first consulting with your medical doctor. The citations and references made in this book are the best possible available at the time of printing. Please refer to *www.boomersrock.us* for any errata or updated editions.

If you have any questions, please contact *support@boomersrock.us.*

This book is dedicated to all who contributed their time and efforts. Without the team, there is no tribe.

To my grandchildren, Harper Ann Schutte and Brecken Henry Schutte, may your Papa Tom's work enable a beautiful future for all of Generation Alpha and beyond!

The future is not shaped by people who don't really believe in the future. It is shaped by men and women who want something very much or believe very much.

John C. Gardner

G.I. GEN • SILENT GEN • BABY BOOMERS
MILLENNIALS • GEN Z • ALPHA
GENERATION US
NEWS
A-F
FAX
VHS
Road Atlas
NETFLIX
WIKIPEDIA
Smart TV
9:24

TABLE OF CONTENTS

PART 4: LEARNING

FOREWORD

By Kerry Hannon

In this anthology, *Generation Us*, Tom Matt shares his powerful voice of experience and the voices of collaborators to help spread a message of acceptance, happiness, independence and empathy. His hand-selected Sherpas provide a commanding launchpad to get each of us thinking about how we can incorporate these ingredients into our own lives to build social connection, mental engagement and meaning into our lives.

There's something about talking to Tom that makes me smile. It revs up my energy. The conversation flows with possibility, hope and the human connection.

Each time I have the opportunity to talk with Tom, I'm reminded of his utter sincerity and his innate curiosity about the challenges we all face in life. His stated focus is on the Baby Boomers, but that is almost always a starting point for him as he probes and discusses the challenges of every generation. We are all going to need help navigating the longer lifespans that are now possible, and we'll need help navigating the unchartered territory of the future.

I've been fortunate to be a guest on Tom's Boomers Rock radio show ten times to discuss my books, including *What's Next?: Finding Your Passion and Your Dream Job in Your Forties, Fifties and Beyond; Love Your Job: The New Rules of Career Happiness,* and *Great Jobs for Everyone 50+: Finding Work That Keeps You Happy and Healthy...and Pays the Bills.* Our discussions have been freewheeling from kibitzing about how to launch a rewarding encore career, to tips on how to take our jobs and love them (not shove them), to ways to find meaningful work that keeps us mentally and physically sharp, and how we can all, regardless of our ages, support each other to create successful journeys.

He generously gives me air time to preach *Kerry's Program of Physical, Financial and Spiritual Fitness* as the three keys to staying relevant, working and giving back as we age; and he echoes my mantra to his listeners:

You need to be fit all around to achieve most things in life– not only a career change or landing a job you love when you're over 50.

My three-part fitness plan encompasses:

PHYSICALLY FIT
When you're physically fit, you have the strength and mental sharpness to deal with stress, especially when changing jobs, or making big decisions. It sounds superficial, but an in-shape and energetic appearance is a bonus in our work and personal lives. It's a great way to combat ageism. It's better than Botox, or dying your hair. You give off a positive, can-do vibe that you're up for the job or project. People want to be around you. They want you on their team.

SPIRITUALLY FIT
Mind-body balance helps you calmly roll with the punches and teaches you to quietly listen to the inner voice that guides your decisions. Meditation practice, yoga, tai chi, or regular long walks with your dog, like I do, can help here.

FINANCIALLY FIT
Economic stability gives you freedom of choice. It provides the nimbleness you need to start a new career,

whether that means opening your own business, paying the tuition to go back to school, or making it easier to work in a job that you love– even if it pays less than your old one. Do a budget. Where can you trim back, pay down debts, downsize? This takes time, but the payback is that it gives you options. Debt is a dream killer.

———

Both Tom and I share with our audiences our deeply held belief in the importance of searching inside when you're making shifts in your life. When I counsel older workers in particular, my refrain is to look at their skill sets and past experiences as transferable to lots of different challenges and fields.

Answer some important questions: What am I best at? What do I love to do? What don't I like to do? Ask friends and colleagues, too. They might see things that you take for granted.

Think of it not as reinventing yourself, but rather as redirecting or redeploying many of the skills you already have in place. This advice, Tom and I agree, is good for all generations.

And we must carry each other from time to time and not be afraid to ask for help. Find a mentor or two, for example, working in a field that interests you. Seek out mentees you've worked with in the past to help guide you to your future. Over time, things shift, and now they may be in a position to help you make your next move.

Finally, do something each day to work toward your goal. Changing careers, or your direction in life, can be nerve-racking. Begin with a mental picture of where you want to go, tape a photograph on your office wall of what it might look like, build out a page on your computer with images found on Pinterest, journal about your goals.

Get things moving by taking small steps. That might mean making a phone call to ask for advice, or reaching out with an e-mail a day to make a lunch date to knock around possibilities. People like to do small favors. And it helps to build a relationship that may lead to your next adventure. Be realistic. Nothing lasts forever.

As you launch into this collection of essays, one line from The Rolling Stones' song *Ruby Tuesday* sticks in my mind, and in fact, was a quote I used in my high school yearbook back in 1978:

Lose your dreams and you will lose your mind.

Take these essays to heart. Take inspiration where offered, and consider the advice when given.

We are all in charge of our own lives, but it's important that we help each other along the way.

Generation Us is about helping each and every one of us, regardless of the name attached to our generation.

KERRY HANNON is a nationally-recognized expert and strategist on career transitions, personal finance and retirement. She is a frequent TV and radio commentator and is a highly sought-after keynote speaker at conferences across the country. She is a frequent contributor to the *New York Times,* and is an award-winning and best-selling author of 12 books.

THE 'POWER OF BE'

Be interested. Be mindful. Be accepting. Be willing to listen, learn and understand. Be open. Be humble. Be compassionate. Be considerate. Be perceptive. Be calm. Be patient. Be hungry. Be proud. Be ready. Be powerful. Be yourself. Be loving. Be encouraging. Be respectful. Be courageous. Be you. Be curious. Be open minded. Be resilient. Be optimistic. Be immersed. Be available. Be inquisitive. Be empathetic. Be present. Be attentive. Be up for it. Be responsible. Be respectful. Be a connector. Be observant. Be synergistic. Be humble. Be excited. Be trustworthy. Be kind. Be focused. Be timely. Be confident. Be transparent. Be involved. Be professional. Be welcoming. Be happy. Be accommodating. Be eager. Be willing. Be engaging. Be insightful. Be observant. Be tolerant. Be articulate. Be intelligent. Be together. Be creative. Be thoughtful. Be good & then great. Be a change agent. Be a team leader. Be a team builder. Be a friend. Be prepared. Be catalytic. Be collaborative. Be Capable. Be friendly. Be balanced. Be prepared. Be gritty. Be principled. Be gregarious. Be clear. Be helpful. Be a teammate. Be intentional. Be a good listener. Be authentic. Be respectful. Be generous. Be understanding. Be secure. Be uplifting. Be purposeful. Be real. Be empowering. Be generous. Be human. Be good. Be aware. Be grateful. Be receptive. Be a mentor.

PART 1

—

INTRODUCTION

PREFACE

By Thomas F. Matt

There is always a story behind the story.

Let me say, right out front, that this book you are about to read almost never came to be. I had no inclination whatsoever to write another book. Frankly, I had convinced myself that focusing on my two lanes (Talk Radio and Public Speaking) was my total emphasis. Many of you may know me, many on the other hand may not, but for those who do, you know that keeping me focused is a challenge of massive proportions. Having written three books and co-authoring another, I was pretty satisfied and ready to stay focused on the two lanes. So much for that!

Here is the story of how the book came to be.

In January of 2017, I was asked to give a keynote for a nursing event in Ann Arbor, Michigan; a very nice event with over 250 nurses from all over Southeast Michigan. At the end of my speech, I was approached and complimented by one of the attendees on the gig. This specific keynote is my go-to speech titled *Ignite Your Life,* which I always customize for each event. This lady's name was Donna Robertson and she worked for the University of Michigan's Survival Flight trauma air flight service, which serves virtually everyone. Donna was interested in discussing my speaking at an event that coming June, but she specifically asked if I could customize a speech about intergenerational relationships in the workplace. The Survival Flight team is comprised primarily of nurses, pilots, support staff and mechanics. Like many other businesses, it sometimes struggles with communication efforts in the workplace. Of course, great productivity is built on relationships and teamwork. In the *Ignite Your Life* keynote I briefly discuss intergenerational relationships and their complexities, as I have an episode on my radio talk show Boomers Rock titled *Building the Bridge*, where I bring Millennials into the studio to talk about this topic. This was not the first time this topic had come up in regard to the *Ignite* keynote. Sometimes audience participants of the seminar would ask the question directly in my Q&A, typically something like "What do you suggest to improve communication between older and younger workers? We are just not getting along that well."

So the seed of this book was growing. With the radio program *Building the Bridge* episodes, this idea was about to get a shot of Miracle-Gro fertilizer. *Generation Us* was bound to happen.

At the same time, I was working with a group at Michigan State University on an idea I had pitched to the Dean of the College of Communication Arts and Sciences, Prabu David, and my former Graduate advisor and now Chair of the Media & Information Department, Johannes Bauer. The idea was for a technology summit/symposium, which at that time had no title and was strictly another one of my pitch/dreams. They liked the thought of pairing younger developers (students) and the older population (the Boomers Rock crowd), the buyers of tech and other services into the future. So they introduced me to Dr. Shelia Cotten, a sociologist tech guru at Communication Arts and I had to pitch her on this tech/summit/symposium event thing. She was game, but rather reluctant due to her already-packed schedule.

You see, my two lanes of talk radio and speaking were happening, and I was bound and determined to learn how to produce large, live events. I had no idea the depth of what it takes to produce a live event within the auspices of an institution like MSU. Thank goodness for Shelia and her assistant from Sparrow Hospital, Sharon Baer.

So basically, I have a lot of irons in the fire... typical of my life. (I like it this way!) The bottom line was I needed a title to my live event, so the *Generation Us* theme came to me like a lightning bolt. Honestly, I have been playing with the 'generational' tags for a long time. I mean, I shit-canned the dubious 'mid-life' on the radio program years ago and started to use the terms 'MiddleLiving' (40-85) and 'Superior Seniors' (86+). I knew that the Boomer generation would become dated and that living to 100 with Quality of Life, the demographic of people becoming empty nesters, or being in transitional phases of life was only going to grow larger. Which, in fact, it has– and *Generation Us* seemed kinda cool so I pitched it to the group at MSU for the fall event on a whim. Well guess what? It won by a nose for the title of the fall event.

See how crazy things can happen? I swear it's the serendipitous law of attraction; this stuff happens to me a lot. I still had absolutely zero interest in a book project. I know what it takes to pull these together, and even though I feel like a veteran with three under my belt, well let's say dubious is putting it lightly.

As I started pulling the University of Michigan Survival Flight seminar together, I was booked to do another gig at MSU on the same topic, and they were two days apart, June 4th and June 6th of 2017, respectively, with a panel to speak at on June 2nd. Crazy would be an understatement, but see above where I said this is "typical of my life" and "I like it this way," being a glutton for sharing the word. During this week of speaking, it was dawning on me that this topic had legs, not book legs, but certainly radio content and especially speaking legs. This could be good for our fledgling business. In an entrepreneurial world, one in which many of us may find ourselves, you've gotta be nimble, flexible and ready to pivot.

Basically, this is the story of my life!

Additionally, I've had the golden opportunity to have really smart college students as friends and their input into the process of crafting my speech is totally invaluable. Their input into the speech and the *Power of Be* makes their contributions to this book so respected, it is what makes this whole project super special to me. I love my young friends so much and appreciate their enthusiasm for being included. Frankly, it is amazing!

So several days after the crazy week of June that included four speaking engagements and a huge open house at our home, one of my good friends Chuck Harden asks me out of the blue, "Hey Tom, are you going to do a book on *Generation Us*?"

My immediate answer was, "Umm no way, I'm way too busy, gotta focus on my two lanes." Thank you to Chuck for planting that seed, because overnight, something grew in my head: a book anthology project called *Generation Us*.

The next day, (again, serendipity) I spoke with my friend and mentor Chris Johnson of On Target Living. This is a guy who has been an advocate for our work, always giving inspiration and great positive advice and feedback. I had not spoken to Chris in a couple of months due to his extensive traveling– he is an amazing motivational speaker, global kind of kingpin. I asked Chris his opinion on the writing of this book, as he was aware of me speaking on this topic, and he could not have been more receptive and encouraging. Damn near demanding might be a better way to describe his feedback: "Tom, you gotta do this book!" Well, that sealed that decision.

In the early days of this brand I call Boomers Rock, there was no radio, there was no podcast, no speaking, no books, no blog. Just Sandy and I, and a dream to accomplish something as future empty-nesters. When I did meet with M3 Group in Lansing to discuss branding, I had brought with me two books: Jack Canfield's *Chicken Soup for the Soul* and one of the *Dummies* books. I told my friends at M3 that I wanted to write books like this, especially *Chicken Soup.* I loved the anthology angle of contributors and stories, so I had this seed in my mind for a long time and *Generation Us* is the anthology that I knew I would help create. I had tremendous faith that someday this would happen! Now keep in mind, this meeting was in 2010, so any fledgling entrepreneur/MiddleLiving business wannabe, heed our story. Dreams keep you flourishing, and anyone who knows me can attest I am one 'flourishing cat!'

In the world today, we need to collaborate. We need to

leverage the old-school sense of neighborhood and community, and we need to break down all of these beliefs that have been perpetuated almost out of habit. The time has come for some new ideas and habits.

I see this brand, *Generation Us*, as a vehicle for good, and as a series of books. The potential to influence people, with kindness, with ideas, with communication; is just so exciting that I cannot stand it. Let's become part of the new-new tribe of *Generation Us*, and let's make a lot of noise and have some fun.

INTRODUCTION

By Thomas F. Matt

—

PROBLEM:

Older and Younger Americans are divided by a shared future.

Every generation has had its challenges, and each has found ways to deal with them. So shall we. But who, exactly, is going to solve our shared problems?

We are, of course, and this book is a step towards solving those problems. This book is a chance to embrace the mystery of the future full-on, with all the gusto of our ancestors.

A BIT MORE ABOUT THE PROBLEM

This book is a collection of essays about the soft skills needed to change the world for the better. They have been written by both younger and older people and present ideas on how to face our challenges. These authors were brought together by Tom Matt, founder of the Boomers Rock talk show, who had the idea that the problems of the future weren't going away and aren't going to solve themselves.

Up until 100 years ago, Americans found jobs because businessmen needed cheap labor. Starting around 70 years ago, as American businesses began to dominate world markets, some Americans (but not all) flourished because they provided skilled labor. The Baby Boomers, born after World War II, benefited the most from this recent economic era. But now the world has changed again.

The pain of that change is inflicted most severely on the younger generations. They don't see the bright future that the Baby Boomers have already enjoyed.

The Baby Boomers are a legion, and many of them have arrived at retirement age with money, health benefits and a chance to savor the American dream; but not all of them. The majority of Baby Boomers have little or no retirement. They're afflicted with nagging or chronic illness, and face a grim march into the night.

While the Boomers are turning pages in their lives, the majority of Millennials, many saddled with college debt, are struggling to find jobs with living wages. Career paths seem to lead into a swamp of doubt. Communication is nonstop and keeping up with the Joneses is reaching a fever pitch. This thing called the Internet created a tsunami of lifestyle changes never imagined.

Americans in between these two generations (Boomers and Millennials) are faced with worry about their future. Many are sandwiched between parents with expensive health problems and children struggling to leave the nest. As the pressure of automation and globalization constrain wage growth, some younger Americans blame the Baby Boomers for squandering economic growth that can no longer be sustained. They're leaving nothing behind for the future generations.

And those Baby Boomers, without resources of their own, many of whom expected government programs to act as a safety net, blame the younger generations for not working hard enough to keep things going as they once were.

All of this is exacerbated by a widening gap between the wealthiest Americans and everyone else. It seems unlikely that the haves will be sharing anything with the have-nots anytime soon. It seems anyone without resources to care for themselves must reach out for help to enjoy the future.

But who will help them?

In the land of opportunity, there's no reason any American can't find a way to reinvent themselves and improve their life. Is 'American Exceptionalism' still viable? In the country known for invention, innovation and a dynamic marketplace to support both, Americans should be able to create their own luck and seize the opportunities to improve their life.

But how do you pull off that trick?

The answer lies in connecting the experience and knowledge of older Americans with the technical skills and eagerness of younger Americans. However, our culture is rooted in a tradition of strict hierarchy, where workers advance through the ranks of a company, earning more pay as their responsibilities increase. That tradition is threatened the most by automation-eliminating jobs, and globalization transferring many more overseas to take advantage of cheaper labor.

Young Americans see nowhere to go with their career just as older Americans see their own jobs disappear. In urban areas, there are often service jobs available, but those rarely provide the same level of wage as manufacturing or other skilled labor. In smaller communities, where a single, anchor employer acts as the local economic engine, the effects of eliminating jobs are devastating, as there is not even the possibility of shifting to service jobs.

We must find a way to connect the dispossessed and teach them to teach each other how to solve problems, build businesses and create value. That's what *Generation Us* is all about. We are a people, young and old, who face a shared problem. We may want to blame each other for the problem, but that won't help. We must find a way to use our differences as an advantage. We must help each other, trust each other and rely on each other to improve our lives.

INTRODUCING 'GENERATION US'

The soft skills in life are what will get us through the 21st century– skills like love, communication, empathy and gratitude make all the difference, to everyone, in dealing with life's challenges. As described in Dr. Daniel Goleman's book, *Emotional Intelligence*, there are social-emotional skills that are the key to success in this world. Right now, those skills are in high demand. Our world is thrashing at the problems we face, and we're not making the progress we need.

I started the *Generation Us* movement after feedback from several speaking engagements led me to the intergenerational approach to problem solving. In my various roles at Michigan State University, not least of which was a non-traditional student earning an advanced degree, I regularly interacted with several generations of problem-solvers while also raising two daughters and witnessing the challenges the world presented to them.

I'm concerned about the future, and I believe *Generation Us* will make the future brighter. Central to *Generation Us* is *The Power of Be,* a collection of positive attitudes for dealing with problems.

I hope you'll keep an open mind and an open heart as you read these essays. Let the flood of ideas bring you hope, and don't hesitate to make changes in your life for the better.

The world needs your best self now more than ever. You owe it to yourself, and the future, to make positive changes wherever and whenever you can.

Peace.

ABOUT THE AUTHORS

Debbie Heiser (Be a Mentor) is a great friend and an even better guest on the radio show, having been on over twenty times! I feel proud to call her a friend; she is one of the most amazing people I know. My thanks to her for contributing this piece.

Samantha Medved (Be Respectful) is and has become a great friend who just happens to be a college student at Michigan State. Her collaboration in my many ideas is and has been challenging and heartfelt: challenging in that I have learned a lot about communication with the younger generations via social media, email, etc. from her; and heartfelt because this kid has game and is going places. I am happy to call her my friend. Thank you, Sam, for taking the time to submit this. I knew you had it in you!

I met **Dr. Deb Feltz** (Be Curious) when I was a participant in her *Train Like an Astronaut* study at MSU, six months of riding an exercise bike, six days a week, against a computer-generated avatar that you could never beat. She is a giver who has helped thousands of students at MSU as a Distinguished Professor in/former Chair of Kinesiology. I thank her for her advice and contributions to the radio program and to this book.

Dave Hornak, Ed. D (Be Happy & Grateful) is a guy who walks the walk and runs the walk and then sprints the message! A great friend and collaborator, all he ever does is give back, and for that I love his juice! His work as Superintendent of Holt Public Schools is a testament to his love for the kids. That is why I wanted him in on this project– he has the 'It' quality. Thank you Dave for submitting this piece.

Debbie Jamieson (Be Proactive), a practicing Clinical Nutritionist since 1979, is a lady who is probably THE nicest person you will ever meet. Always smiling, humble, giving and just plain cool. Sandy and I just love having her on the radio program as a guest. I am privileged to call her my friend and her husband, Dr. Thomas Jamieson, is my personal physician. Thanks Deb for writing this *Be*-ism!

Colin Milner (Be Happy/Be Prepared) is CEO of the International Council on Active Aging and founder of the active-aging industry in North America. A leading authority on the health and well-being of older adults, Milner has been recognized by the World Economic Forum as one of "the most innovative and influential minds" on topics related to aging. The award-winning writer has authored more than 300 articles. Milner has been published in such journals as Global Policy and the Annual Review of Gerontology and Geriatrics. He also contributed a chapter to the World Economic Forum's book, *Global Population Aging: Peril or Promise?*

Bill Kost (Be Flexible) and I have known each other for many years now, as we both work at MSU. We have become best buds in the past few years as I train him and he helps me. I came up with the term 'Cerebral Workout' out of respect to our yakking at the gym and not really pushing much weight around. A great man, husband and dad, he is a good dude who wants to help others, and for that I am grateful for his contribution.

Colin Jackson (Be Empathetic) is one of the most talented and humble young men I know. He is the most self-effacing gentleman ever. I thought it interesting and cool to have the dual perspectives of a younger man/ Millennial and myself. Thank you, Colin, for this submission– it made me tear up, truthfully!

Lisa Cini (Be a Coach) is new to our collective family as of this writing, but I see greatness in her and her boundless desire to make a difference. When we had our very first phone call, a pre-production visit for the radio program, I knew immediately that she was special. Her episode reflected that, and made evident her desire to contribute this piece. She knocked this out in less than a week. I look forward to more collaborative work with Lisa and I thank her for her contribution.

Sky Bergman (Be Yourself) is an accomplished, award-winning photographer and Professor of Photography and Video at Cal Poly State University in San Luis Obispo, CA. As a guest on our radio program, Sky is a super-charged energizer bunny, which fits well in our world. Her film, *Lives Well Lived*, celebrates the incredible wit, wisdom and experiences of adults aged 75 to 100 years old. It is Sky's directorial debut. This is a bad-ass film and everyone should see it. To learn more about *Lives Well Lived,* visit the website at *www.lives-well-lived.com.*

Nick Tijerina (Be Creative) is a colleague and coworker of mine at MSU and has been very influential in my life. He is the person who first introduced me to the Intramural Facilities at MSU in 2000, for that I am very grateful as it completely changed my life. Because he's a very creative soul, I wanted Nick to share some of his art, poetry, and this submission which he did. Ironically enough, his submission is titled *Be Creative.* Thank you Nick for being my friend and for your work.

Brandon Townsend (Be Passionate) is a current student at MSU. When I met Brandon for the first time, he was working at IM West, the gym where I train. Brandon is an old soul in a young man's body who has tremendous work ethic, and he just gets it. We have had many discussions on his major of Kinesiology and Human Nutrition. When he commits, he gets it done, and for a young man in his early 20s, he is not a social media honk like so many of his peers. What does that tell you? Thanks Brandon for coming through on your deliverable and for being a good guy. Be Passionate– we all need to follow your advice.

Mike Secord (Be Powerful, Be Proud) The story of my friendship and admiration of Mike Secord is too lengthy for this forum. I have known Mike for over ten years and never have I seen him be grumpy or short with people. His story of fighting cancer is a gift to this book and his interview on the radio program was so bad-ass that it makes me get emotional just thinking about it. When you think you got it bad, read Mike's story. Thank you, Mike, for contributing and for being you! Love you bro! Be Powerful, Be Proud– I wish we all had this man's heart!

1923

By Thomas F. Matt

It is my belief that 97 percent of the people work for the three percent of the people who never gave up.
Daniel Millstein

Ageism runs rampant and is steaming hot, with headlines constantly shouting about workplace warfare and anxiety between generations, younger people who doubt themselves, doubt older adults and doubt the system. Older adults doubt themselves, doubt younger adults and they doubt the system. See a pattern?

To be sure there are ample reasons that people have these feelings: Baby Boomers lost jobs and trillions of retirement income in the great recession, forcing them to work longer than they planned and creating a trickle-down of anxiety for our children who are the Millennials. Millennials stayed in our homes, not earning enough out of high-school/college, embodying the 'failure to launch' model into their own independent adult life. Mix into the steaming stewpot caregiving for older adult parents of the Boomers, and we have the right recipe for interdependency never seen before. How did we get here?

Our current frame of life starts with its increased longevity. Since 1900, our society has added an additional 30 years of life.[1] Wow, now that can build some change in planning! The United States Census Bureau estimates that the number of Americans living into their nineties will quadruple between 2010 and 2050.[2] Unfortunately, due to flawed expectations which are rooted in what I refer to on the radio program as a '1950s mentality,' these additional years give rise to anxiety and cultural seismic shifts. The additional years that we have added to our collective lives are not just tacked on to the generational belief of '65 and out.' Rather, they are distributed throughout life stages, stretching our beliefs and actions.

Young Adulthood (18-39), MiddleLiving (40-85) and Superior Seniors (86+) are all being transformed, yet still follow a generational mindset– rooted deep, in a well of dark water, held in a 1950s bucket. How will this work to our benefit, and how do we leverage the 'stretching' of living?

Welcome to *Generation Us*– the 21st century is here and we have a plan.

I really thought that before we do the deep dive of writing a shopping list of where and what we are all going to do together, I needed to step back and define how we arrived at this train stop. Where did the generations and generational segmentation thinking begin? The answer, everyone, is 1923! Time capsule gang, many people who read my books have told me they like the time capsule thinking and my crazy bouncing around. When your brain works in overdrive pretty much 200% of the time, it makes editors crazy and chapters short.

The year 1923 had many moments that would distinguish it as an important year.

For example:

JANUARY 1ST

Southern Cal defeated Penn State 14-3 in The Rose Bowl.

FEBRUARY 13TH

Organization of the 1st Black Professional Basketball team, *the Renaissance*

MARCH 2ND

The first issue of Time magazine was published.

MARCH 26TH

The Ottawa Senators defeated the Vancouver Millionaires (later known as the Maroons) 3 games to 1 for the Stanley Cup (PCHA).

APRIL 18TH

The first Yankee Stadium opened its doors in the Bronx, New York City.

MAY 28TH

Attorney General declared it legal for women to wear trousers.

MAY 28TH

U.S. unemployment nearly ended.

JUNE 9TH

Brinks unveiled the its first of its armored vans.

JULY 13TH

The famous Hollywood sign was inaugurated in California, reading 'Hollywoodland.' The last four letters would be dropped in 1949.

AUGUST 2ND

Vice President Calvin Coolidge becomes the 30th President of the United States upon the death of President Warren G. Harding.

SEPTEMBER 1ST

A 7.9-magnitude earthquake strikes Tokyo and Yokohama, killing 142,000.

OCTOBER 6TH

The first National League unassisted triple play (Ernie Padgett, Braves vs. Phillies)

OCTOBER 15TH

The New York Yankees won their first world series, beating the New York Giants 4 games to 2.

OCTOBER 16TH

Roy and Walt Disney founded the *Disney Brothers Cartoon Studio.*

DECEMBER 3RD

The first U.S. Congressional open session was broadcasted on radio.

DECEMBER 31ST

The first transatlantic radio broadcast: Pittsburgh, PA to Manchester, England

Additionally,

- The Roaring Twenties were still in full swing
- Prohibition was in effect and would be until 1930
- The population of the U.S. was just under 112 million.[3]

Also in 1923, Sociologist Karl Mannheim would inadvertently begin the segmentation of generations of the 20th century with his paper, *The Problem of Generations.*

Yes, 1923 was a defining year!

Karl Mannheim's 1923 essay *The Problem of Generations* has been described by some as the determining paper that established generational boundaries, and that the difference of an age group is determined by historical occurrences. Karl Mannheim is known as one of the founding fathers of the sociology of knowledge. He put forth the notion that all truths and ideas are related to, and inclined by, the social circumstances in which they come from.

Mannheim's research and writings led to the *Theory of Generations.* That theory led to the belief that the social context of a generation is built upon older generations. Historical occurrences, as defining moments, would lead to the segmentation of twenty year windows. So in essence this is where the story of *Generation Us* begins. Thanks to a Hungarian Sociologist, the world was forever broken into age demographics. That is, until now, thanks in part to the proliferation of the Internet.[4]

Now, we welcome *Generation Us!*

THE SEVEN EXISTING GENERATIONS OF THE 20TH AND 21ST CENTURIES:

1. The G.I. Generation – *Born 1901-1924*
2. The Silent Generation – *Born 1925-1945*
3. Baby Boomers – *Born 1946-1964*
4. Generation X – *Born 1965-1979*
5. Generation Y (Millennials) – *Born 1980-1995*
6. Generation Z – *Born 1996-2013*
7. Generation Alpha – *Born 2014 and on*

Before we can solve a problem, we have to define it. A

generation has been defined as a group of individuals born and living contemporaneously. The members of each generation share special qualities, spreading knowledge/ practices that can affect thoughts, beliefs, behaviors and values. These collective experiences influence our outlooks, actions and mindsets. They also mold our ideas about company loyalty, work ethic and the definition of a job well done. And now that five different generations are working together simultaneously, from the G.I. Generation to Generation Z and beyond, it's even more important to understand where everyone's coming from.

Much is made of the supposedly distinct generations that have existed since the Second World War. The Baby Boomers, who grew up through the swinging sixties, were studied in great detail as demographers wondered just how well-to-do this post-war group could be. Generation X, born in the late sixties and seventies were raised amid an explosion in mass media and thus came to be dubbed 'The MTV Generation.' Then there are the Millennials, whose attitudes and desires have been the subject of many thousands of press articles, research papers and conferences over the past few years.

Much of what is said is nonsense. We're all individuals and few people fall directly into the stereotypes associated with their generation. In fact, many of the characteristics associated with Millennials, particularly that they are work-shy and ungrateful, have been ascribed to 20-somethings of every generation. But understanding what makes people tick at a certain age is valuable – both for marketers who want to sell them stuff, and for managers who want to hire them.

THE G.I. GENERATION: 1901-1924

Although many of this generation have passed, their influences still affect many of the systems and beliefs of today. Members of this generation include:

- U.S. President John F. Kennedy
- Television anchor Walter Cronkite
- Baseball Hall-of-Famer Lou Gehrig
- Actor Jimmy Stewart

When I share this presentation with groups in my live events, I like to show the audience a picture of Jimmy Stewart and mention his classic film *It's a Wonderful Life*. Jimmy plays George Bailey, who, through a series of events, finds himself in a pickle with the film's villain Henry Potter (Lionel Barrymore). Consistently, many of the Millennial generation attendees have never seen or heard of Jimmy Stewart or seen the film. Yes, to me it seems outrageous, but to them, well, never heard of him.

The Greatest Generation is a term made popular by journalist Tom Brokaw to describe the generation who grew up in the United States during the deprivation of the Great Depression, and then went on to fight in World War II; as well as those whose productivity within the war's home front made a decisive, material contribution to the war effort. The term has become synonymous with the G.I. Generation.[5]

INFLUENTIAL HISTORICAL AND SOCIAL EVENTS OF THE G.I. GENERATION

- World War I, 1914-1918
- The Boy Scouts formed in 1910, Girl Scouts in 1912

- Prohibition, 1919-1930
- The beginning of the Roaring Twenties
- Legislation to protect children and child labor laws
- The sinking of the Titanic in 1912
- Kellogg's Corn Flakes sold for the first time in 1906 & Oreo cookies in 1912

THE SILENT GENERATION: 1925-1946

The oldest (for the most part) living generation in American culture is the Silent Generation. They lived during the dark years of the Great Depression (1929-1939) and many either fought or were children during World War II.[6] The hardships of war and the economy deeply affected this generation's values and opinions in regard to many issues. For example, family, religion, work ethic, government and patriotism were a few of beliefs and values of this generation, shaping their collective mindsets.

Resourcefulness and the stretching of very limited assets was influenced by the effects of the Great Depression and the New Deal in prompting economic recovery. Understanding the journey and history helps to pave empathy and enlightenment. Empathy will be a massive driver in all of the *Generation Us* book series. Without it, nothing can change.

About 55 million members of the Silent Generation reside in the United States today.[7] Described as being loyal and orderly, this generation values honesty, character and sacrifice; respects authority and values boundaries between family life and work. They are hard workers who developed a self-reliant attitude toward financial security.

INFLUENTIAL HISTORICAL AND SOCIAL EVENTS OF THE SILENT GENERATION[8]

- The Great Depression
- World War II
- Pearl Harbor
- D-Day
- The Korean War
- The Golden Age of Radio
- The rise of labor unions

THE BABY BOOMERS: 1946-1964

The Baby Boomers are one of the largest generational cohorts, comprising an estimated 76 million people. Babies born between 1946 and 1955 were sometimes considered in literature as Early Boomers, and those born between 1956-1964 were the Late Boomers. I fall into the latter category as a 1959 baby. There are important inconsistencies between the earlier boomers and those born later on within that twenty-year timeframe. Looking at the differences between the two subgroups helps paint a stronger picture of a generation that is as complex as it is large. With dramatic changes occuring across the political, social and global landscape, the Baby Boomers can be divided into the Early Boomers generation (teens in the '60s) and Generation Jones (Late Boomers/teens in the '70s).

During the Boomer years, a baby was born every eight seconds. Certainly, the title 'Baby Boom' was appropriate for this big generation of 76 million. By 1964, Boomers comprised 40% of the U.S. population.

The tag lines and generational names that have continued

to perpetuate this distinct labeling of people and generations are a key driver to why I wanted to speak on this topic and write about it. More than ever, I am convinced that Professor Mannheim would be shocked to see what time and marketing did to his theory of generations.

EARLY BOOMERS

Early Boomers grew up as the world was wildly shifting. They were inspired by the changing role of women, the new commercial landscape and the rise of a counter-culture that was strong-minded enough to leave a lasting impression on the world. These Early Boomers were inspired to act by those they saw standing up for change. They admired, followed and fought with the likes of Martin Luther King Jr, Gloria Steinem and JFK. These Early Boomers were committed to reexamining the Traditionalist worldview and changing the world they lived to reveal values inspired by their youth-driven counterculture. The thought process and tagline 'never trust anyone over 30' became a mainstay of this hippie generation as stated by Jack Weinberg in the 1960s.[9]

INFLUENTIAL HISTORICAL AND SOCIAL EVENTS OF THE EARLY BOOMERS[10]

- Woodstock
- The Vietnam War
- The Civil Rights Movement
- The Women's Rights movement
- The Moon Landing

While Early Boomers had major portraits to look up to, Generation Jones was too young to recall these icons in their peak. These Jonesers were too early for Woodstock, the *I have a Dream* speech and the assassination of President Kennedy in November of 1963. The youth-driven counter-culture of the Early Boomer movements had consummated many of its goals. Those young people that had been fighting for change were fighting for career growth by the 1970s. Instead of the idealistic and optimistic outlook of the Early Boomers, Generation Jones was experiencing the backlash of an economy that was falling dramatically. The inflation rate peaked at over 10%, the highest in the century,[11] and I remember long gas lines well. Times were tough.

This economic hardship and slipping post-war optimism defined the atmosphere that Gen Jonesers experienced as they were coming into their formative years.

Life at home was different for all of us, different than the more outmoded setting that Early Boomers experienced. More homes were being forced into having two working parents due to changes in the economy and job availability. When Generation Jones went to school, there were not enough desks or books in the classroom because the school system wasn't ready for this large cohort. They weren't ready to put their kids in the same situation, so families were beginning to shrink in size. 'The pill' became available so birth control and family planning were easier than in the past. With the competitive job market and economic stresses, divorce was on the rise as Gen Jonesers entered their formative years, causing teens to spend more time working individually and caring for themselves.

While this wasn't the generation of latch-key kids, Generation Jones was on the trailing edge of Generation X, which saw a dramatic spike in divorce rate and latch-key kids. This was the time my own parents divorced, while the economy took a nosedive, fuel prices spiked, the oil embargo impacted the nation and job opportunities shrunk. Generation Jones had to become more independent and learn to fight for their future, because they quickly understood that nothing would be handed to them. With the tight job market, they knew they had to put their head down and work hard, dress for the job they wanted (not the job they had), and develop other methods of standing out. This was important for career growth, but at the time the main focus was on simply keeping their jobs. This period of fierce competition for job stability has stayed with Generation Jones, who earned their name by constantly striving to "Keep up with the Joneses" or "Jonesin'" for something more.

INFLUENTIAL HISTORICAL AND SOCIAL EVENTS OF THE LATE BOOMERS[12]

- Watergate
- Stagflation
- The Arab Oil Embargo
- The Iran Hostage Crisis
- Deindustrialization

GENERATION X: 1965-1979

Most members of this cohort are tagged as Gen Xers, Busters and the Lost Generation. Between 46 & 53 million members of this tribe live in the United States.[13] The term Buster refers to the lower birthrate than those of the preceding Boomer generation. The Lost Generation describes this group because it was the first generation of latch-key children: the ones often left at home with insignificant parental direction. These children would be the first to start the daycare revolution, as both parents were working in greater numbers.

It is reported that a lack of meaningful family relationships led Gen Xers to create non-traditional families by bonding with friends and classmates.[14]

Author Jeff Gordinier was tired of being force-fed the Beatles, the Summer of Love, Facebook and Britney Spears, so he wrote a book: *X Saves the World: How Generation X Got the Shaft But Can Still Keep Everything From Sucking.* It's a tongue-in-cheek, passionate book that stimulated age-based discussions in chat rooms, living rooms and offices across the nation.

Gordinier says being heard over the media clamor about Boomers and their progeny, Generation Y (or Millennials as they're now known), isn't just a challenge, it's exasperating. Being ignored and underappreciated is never-ending for him and his tribe of fellow Gen Xers.

Sandwiched between 76 million Baby Boomers and 80 million Millennials, Generation X– roughly defined as anyone born between 1965 and 1980– makes this group's label a dark-horse demographic "condemned by numbers alone to 'nicheville,'" as Gordinier puts it in the book.[15]

Segmenting and discriminating will tend to really tick people off. It is our history, and another case for Professor Mannheim to want to turn over in his grave.

Given their upbringing, it's no surprise that the Busters

(could there be a worse tag?), are as overlooked. How can they be expected to maintain a balance between work and family life? They do not care to work the long hours for the titles or money, and are reportedly less loyal to their employers and more comfortable demanding flexible work arrangements. They expect freedom and balance to be part of their lives.

Considered to be independent, self-reliant and informal, Gen Xers multitask well and like working independently on projects. They prefer to manage their own time, set their own limits and complete work without supervision.[16]

INFLUENTIAL HISTORICAL AND SOCIAL EVENTS OF THE GEN XERS

- First to grow up with cell phones
- Personal computing
- The Challenger Disaster
- The Fall of the Berlin Wall
- The Women's Liberation movement

GENERATION Y: 1980-1995

The people who fall into the Generation Y tribe, also referred to as the Millennials, or sometimes Nexters, comprise the largest of all of the demographic segments, estimated at about 80 million.[17] Having grown up using computers, mobile phones, tablets and other electronic devices, the Millennial population is very technologically-savvy. My oldest daughter Ashley falls into this category. I remember very well watching her as a pre-teen using our first computer with dial-up and AOL, with what seemed like 15 different chat boxes open at once. Amazing to think about now.

Unlike the latch-key kids that were the previous generation, the Gen Y kids were doted over and escorted everywhere. From school events to athletic travel teams, many in this generation had 'helicopter parents'– parents who were involved in every aspect of their children's lives. I fall into this category, and also am guilty of the active enabling of the 'participation award,' where every kid received an award just for showing up, and the concept of winning was marginalized by losing.

Reported as being easily bored and impatient, this generation is motivated by a sense of purpose and belonging to a meaningful community. They typically enjoy experimenting and discovering different approaches to problems.[18]

Millennials play a highly critical role for businesses moving forward in the 21st century. Millennials offer unique skills– fresh ideas, adaptability and tech-savviness– that businesses need in order to innovate and remain competitive.[19]

More than one-third of American workers today are part of Generation Y. They surpassed Generation X in 2015 to become the largest share of the American workforce, according to Pew Research Center study of U.S. Census Bureau data. This milestone occurred in the first quarter of 2015. The 53.5-million-strong Millennial workforce has risen rapidly. The Baby Boomer labor force, in decline as more Boomers retire, was also surpassed by that of the Millennials last year.[20]

U.S. Labor Force by Generation, 1995-2015

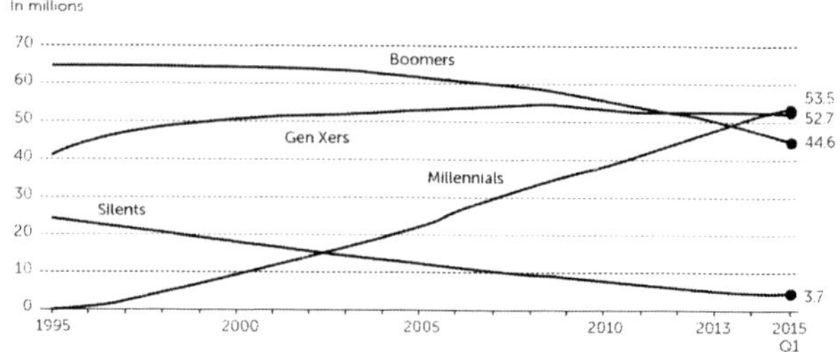

Note: Annual averages plotted 1995-2014. For 2015 the first quarter average of 2015 is shown. Due to data limitations Silent generation is overestimated from 2008-2015.
Source: Pew Research Center tabulations of monthly 1995-2015 Current Population Surveys, Integrated Public Use Microdata Series (IPUMS)

Pew Research Center

INFLUENTIAL HISTORICAL AND SOCIAL EVENTS OF THE MILLENNIALS

- Computers and technology
- Girl's movement
- Rise of social media (Myspace, Friendster, Facebook)
- Google's founding as a search engine
- School yard violence (Columbine, etc.)
- Diversity
- Busy planned lives[21]

GENERATION Z: 1996-2013

While you may still be coming to grips with Millennials, soon you'll be rubbing elbows with their successors. Generation Z members are generally defined as those aged under 20 and are sometimes referred to as post-millennials or the Homeland Generation. Here are a few things you should know about them, mostly courtesy of a new report by M&C Saatchi:

THEY'RE TRUE DIGITAL NATIVES

Millennials spent their formative years perfecting their

Myspace page and playing Snake on their Nokia 3310, but only Generation Z can't remember a time before the internet was ubiquitous. For them, touch screens and social media are as normal as running water. 24% describe themselves as being online "almost constantly," according to a report by the Pew Research Center (then again, plenty of email-addicted execs in their 30s, 40s and 50s would probably say the same).

THEY'VE GROWN UP AROUND TURMOIL

Remember the heady days of the '90s, after the fall of the Berlin Wall but before 9/11, back when Tony Blair assured us that Things Can Only Get Better? Generation Z doesn't. For them, the War on Terror and its associated anxiety about security and the West's place in the world is the norm. They've grown up amid the financial crisis and the economic stagnation that has followed it. These first two factors seem to have shaped many of their more specific characteristics.

THEY'RE RISK-AVERSE

Many-a-'90s (and earlier) teenager enjoyed nothing more than slamming a bottle of vodka, puffing on a few Marlboro Lights (or perhaps something more illicit) at their local park, and generally making a nuisance of themselves. Drug and alcohol consumption among today's youth is well down compared to prior generations. While that might be good for their health, M&C Saatchi suggests Gen Z's aversion to risk runs deeper than that: "Spontaneity, frivolity and making mistakes (the lifeblood of the young to date) has been replaced by a generation of serious-minded strivers, anxious about a challenging future."

THEY'RE MORE SENSIBLE WITH MONEY

"This might be the area in which they differ from Millennials the most," says Goldman Sachs analyst Christopher Wolf. "Millennials are often cast as the 'follow your dreams at all costs' generation. Gen Zers are decidedly more conservative– they're more worried about the rising cost of college and taking on debt." 60% of the Gen Z population believe that having a lot of money in the bank and less debt is evidence of success, compared to 44% of Millennials at the same age. "This is a generation that's really focused on the financial consequences of their decisions," according to Wolf.

So perhaps it's no surprise that they, in the words of M&C Saatchi, like to 'dream small.' Gone are aspirations of owning a fleet of expensive sports cars and a home in Beverly Hills. Today's young are more likely to want a solid job and a modest home. If you're selling something frivolous, don't expect them to part with their cash very easily.

THEY'RE VERY COMPETITIVE

Whether it's the pursuit of wealth or shares and likes on social media, post-millennials are keen to get ahead of their peers. That's reflected in their attitude to work– 70% think they will have to work a lot harder than their parents to reach the same heights– and in how they Instagram and Snapchat everything they do. According to the report, "It's no longer ok to be seen wasting the weekend in bed as teenagers have traditionally done. They need to be seen as being active; out there, having amazing experiences."

THEY DON'T DEAL WITH FLUFF

It's a lot tougher to hold someone's attention when the next piece of information is a tiny touchscreen-swipe away. If you're trying to communicate with Gen Z people, you should get to the point. The report suggests they're cynical of companies with a purpose, preferring down-to-earth pragmatism to "high-minded moral crusading."

So, to recap probably one of my longest chapters ever, here is what we've got, gang...

ALPHAS

- Birth to 17 years old

YOUNG ADULTS

- 18-39 years old
- Are taking longer to enroll & finish their educations
- Are waiting longer to marry
- Are waiting longer to have children
- Are dealing with educational debt

MIDDLELIVING ADULTS

- 40-85 years old
- Are changing careers and directions
- Are retraining and educating themselves more
- Are the largest entrepreneurial group by far
- Are taking time off for sabbaticals and recharging

SUPERIOR SENIORS

- 86+ years old
- Are continuing to add value by mentoring or working part-time
- Are remarrying
- Are taking classes and staying educated
- Are exercising and traveling
- Are living longer and better and are riding the wave!

REFERENCES

1. *www.statenews.com/2017/02/14/living-longer-living-better-aging/*

2. *www.census.gov/content/dam/Census/library/publications/2011/acs/acs-17.pdf*

3. *www.onthisday.com*

4. *www.prezi.com*

5. *https://en.wikipedia.org/wiki/Greatest_Generation*

6. *www.questia.com/library/journal/1P3-3971765321/generations-do-differ-best-practices-in-leading-traditionalists*

7. Ibid

8. *www.veterinaryteambrief.com/article/facing-generational-differences-understanding-key*

9. *www.berkeleydailyplanet.com/issue/2000-04-06/article/759*

10. *www.generations.com/2015/11/09/early-boomers-generation-jones-meet-the-two-boomer-subgroups/*

11. *www.federalreserve.gov/pubs/ifdp/2004/799/ifdp799.htm*

12. Ibid

13. *www.pewresearch.org/fact-tank/2015/05/11/millennials-surpass-gen-xers-as-the-largest-generation-in-u-s-labor-force/*

14. *www.ngenperformance.com/pdf/white/ManagingGenDivide.Overview.pdf*

15. *http://content.time.com/time/arts/article/0,8599,1731528,00.html*

16. *https://www.researchgate.net/publication/229008693_Generational_diversity_What_nurse_managers_need_to_know*

17. *www.ngenperformance.com/pdf/white/ManagingGenDivide.Overview.pdf*

18. Ibid

19. *www.elance-odesk.com/millennial-majority-workforce*

20. *www.pewresearch.org/fact-tank/2015/05/11/millennials-surpass-gen-xers-as-the-largest-generation-in-u-s-labor-force/*

21. *https://managementisajourney.com/15-influential-events-that-shaped-generation-y-infographic/*

———

PART 2

LIVING

DREAMS OF YOU

By N.S. Tijerina

I saw you in my dream last night.
You were like a red and yellow butterfly.
You smelled of lavender and felt of silk.
Your smile was pure joy.
Your eyes were happiness, at least to me.
You touched me as if you were already a part of me.

I saw you in my dream last night.
You were different this time.
You were almost my size.
You hugged me so hard you picked me up.
We were in a place by ourselves.
You said, "Let's do it right here.
Stick that thing in me right now!"
I was a little scared.

I saw you in my dream last night.
You were tall and slender,
Dark brown hair and eyes,
Perfect cream-colored skin,
Your eyes were full of anticipation
Your smile was nervous, a little scared.
You looked at me as if
You wanted to get by me
Sorry if I scared you

You came to me in my dream last night
Or maybe I came to you in yours
We were playing like nervous lovers
We'd get close then move away
The balance of staying or going was
Just one grain of sand on the balance beam
Of our caring for each other
I grabbed you close
held my head to your chest
You said "don't, that is for my next lover"
Those seven words were that grain of sand
Leveraging the scale
In an instant, my heart was gone
Like a butterfly I flitted away
Not to find another flower
But to fly away, to feel my wings again.

TELEVISION AND SPONGEBOB & FRIENDS

By Colin Jackson

——

Life's short. Anything could happen and it usually does, so there is no point in sitting around thinking about all the ifs, ands and buts.
Amy Winehouse

——

I can honestly say television has probably influenced my life as much as any real-life experience. TV has allowed me to bond with so many different people that I either have come to love or had already loved. In the digital age, screens surround us. Though I wasn't alive, I'm sure children that grew up during the advent of television felt a similar love for their magic boxes. In my own experience, most of my memories are tied with television in some way, shape or form.

When I was a baby and wouldn't sleep, my mom sat me on her knee and reclined while we watched *Late Night with Conan O'Brien.* As a little kid, I climbed into my parents' bed in the mornings to watch *Sesame Street* with my mom before pre-school. I would sit on my thinking chair and think when *Blue's Clues* prompted. *Spongebob Squarepants* came out in 1999 and excited me so much, I wrote a note to myself so I wouldn't forget the title when I told my parents about it. Previously, I saw kids on TV on *The Amanda Show* and tried poorly to explain it to my parents. I asked if I could be on as well. The name of the show escaped me and they thought I was imagining things. Other times, things I saw on TV made me mistreat my own TV set. One day in school, we saw an episode of *Bill Nye: The Science Guy* where he dragged a magnet across the screen to show the image distort. Not knowing the damage would be permanent, I went home and immediately had my own science experiment.

In 2008, once my niece and nephew were born, we frequently spent Sundays with them at my brother and sister-in-law's house. That often led to me holding my months-old nephew and simultaneously watching the Detroit Lions play on the living room television. I promised my nephew each week that he'd see the Lions win once before he turned one. The first ever 0-16 season in NFL history caused me to break the first promise I ever made to a baby. More importantly, television was an excuse to come close to people I didn't know much else about.

For a period, my middle brother lived with us while he worked in Lansing. Due to an age gap, I didn't know that much about him. I did know he liked *The Simpsons,* so I would always try to look over his shoulder when he would watch the show on his laptop. This grew into me getting into the groove of watching America's favorite yellow family weekdays at 6:30 p.m. on Fox 47 and new episodes Sundays at 8 p.m. I even bought DVD collections of seasons 4, 5 and 7. *King of the Hill,* a show of which I can honestly say I've seen every episode at least 5 times, followed at 7 p.m. on ABC 53. Then, 7:30 p.m. hit, and we knew it was time for *Jeopardy!* where my mom and I could shout the answers at the screen. She once joked she didn't want to give birth to me until after Jeopardy was finished. It makes sense.

Of course, we bonded as a family outside of the living room. I don't want to create the image of three couch potatoes basing their lives around television. That wasn't the case. We had vacations, trips to the beach, days at the zoo, bike rides, basketball and baseball games and everything else one would imagine. I'm grateful for all those memories. Television just happened to become a reference point I tied memories to. Some of the best ones included watching reruns of my mom's favorite shows on *TV Land.*

Part of the American dream that G.I.'s returning home from WWII/Korea bought into included that beautiful suburban life complete with a loving wife, two kids, a dog, a lawn to mow and a TV to watch after a hard day at work. Once flicking on that TV, they saw a reflection of that very dream they bought into in the form of sitcoms like *Leave it to Beaver.* Although we've never specifically talked about it, I imagine this was my mom's life to an extent. She grew up in Detroit. Her father served in WWII, went to school on the G.I. Bill and worked as an IRS agent. Her mother worked as a teacher in Detroit Public Schools until she retired.

It always amazes me how well she remembers every commercial jingle from slogans used to sell *Nutter Butter* bars to the Detroit Tigers World Series theme song, *Go Get 'Em Tigers.* We whistle the *Andy Griffith Show* theme music together. I must've seen every episode of *I Love Lucy, The Andy Griffith Show, Leave it to Beaver, Sanford and Son, The Jeffersons* and others just by spending summer mornings on the couch watching reruns. *Gilligan's Island, I Dream of Genie* and *Bewitched* also edged into the mix but not as much.

Before dinner, my dad and I watched *Around the Horn.* Afterward, we watched *Pardon the Interruption* from the DVR. This was my introduction to sports broadcasts and journalism. ESPN used to run this *SportsCenter* ad that involved people effectively talking out of their rear ends because they had missed last night's game or the latest sports topics. Dad would jab at me because, still new to the sports world, I would have similar opinions as the people in the ads. Since I now work in sports radio, I guess I should give credit to those days for building my interest in the athletics world and showing me how many different angles it can encompass.

Lately, we've been watching some of my favorite shows. My mom doesn't enjoy them but my dad finds them amusing. Whenever I have the remote, I prefer to watch *South Park, Archer,* or anything on the channel *VICELAND.* Each of these grew from my late-night television habit, which started in 7th grade once I got my first television in my room. I would mute the sound and read the subtitles of every show on *Comedy Central* from 11 p.m. when *The Daily Show* came on until 3 a.m. when the *Girls Gone Wild* commercials really picked up and reruns of *Insomniac with Dave Attell* would air.

I've been considering how my taste in television shows reflects my family. My oldest brother used to stay up late watching Adult Swim shows. I remember whenever we would go over his house, he'd show my dad a random show like *Aqua Teen Hunger Force* or *Super Jail.* Without my oldest brother, I probably wouldn't have given as much attention to Adult Swim shows. In all honesty, I rarely watch them live even today. I binge-watched *The Boondocks* when episodes were on Netflix. My dad and I watched *Black Jesus.* Despite short episodes, *Rick and Morty* always reflects quality. These shows show me that I share a sense of humor with my brother– a fact my dad reminds me of whenever I control the remote. Despite the 17-year age gap, I suppose some similarities still shine through.

Many parts of my life have served as bridges for me to connect with others. Music has influenced my life probably secondmost outside of real life experiences, yet it just seemed right to write about television. Books may stimulate our minds. Music may force us to imagine. Films may have first class production value and plotlines. Theater and sporting events may bring us irreplaceable memories. Still, television, in its gorgeous simplicity, is there for us when we need it. Across the generations, many of us can relate. Not only does it create shared experiences, but also shares foreign perspectives. United, these two join lives together. That, truly, is magic.

OUR GENERATION GAP

By Thomas F. Matt

IN•TER•GEN•ER•A•TION•AL
COL•LAB•O•RA•TION

noun

ENCOURAGING TRUST AND TEAMWORK BETWEEN PEOPLE OF AT LEAST TWO DIFFERENT GENERATIONS THROUGH THE USE OF OPEN AND EFFECTIVE COMMUNICATION BY ALL PARTIES INVOLVED

When I was growing up in the '60s and '70s, being what is now referred to as a Late Boomer, I vividly remember the 'generation gap' being splashed all over the media. Of course, back then, media was limited to our local newspaper, Walter Cronkite sharing the Vietnam War and this new thing called FM radio. What we did have was vinyl records, 8-track tapes, cassettes and rock and roll. It started to change in the '50s, when television began portraying teenagers as juvenile delinquents (James Dean, black leather and denim, fast cars and, of course, loud music). Elvis became King, the Beatles invaded and Motown was more than cars. We were cutting edge, just ask our parents.

Although some generational dissimilarity has existed throughout the past, modern generational breaks have often been attributed to rapid cultural change, particularly with respect to matters such as musical tastes, fashion, culture and politics. These variations are assumed to have been magnified by the unprecedented size of the younger crowd in the 1960s– the largest in history, with 76 million having been born between 1946 and 1964. These numbers gave power and inclination to rebel against societal norms, as reflected in songs such as The Who's 1965 hit *My Generation* and Bob Dylan's *The Times They Are a-Changin'.* 'Make love, not war' resonated with our generation. I may have been a little bit young to have actually been involved in the hippie movement, but I remember it well. (See above– Walter Cronkite!)

Mantras such as 'Don't trust anyone over 30' and 'Tell it like it is' were chronicled in Time Magazine on January 6th, 1967, where it was stated, "The young seem curiously unappreciative of the society that supports them." At that point in time, boomers were called 'alienated' or 'uncommitted,' and there was a sense of mistrust of the 'establishment.' There existed tremendous pressure to excel in school, get into college or face a draft that would likely send young men to the jungles of Vietnam. The war of our time was a lightning rod for the mistrust of 'The Man.'

In the mid-'60s the 'hippies' emerged as a subculture of America, and the 'generation gap' was in full, explosive bloom. The following excerpt, from Time Magazine's July 7th, 1967 issue, identifies and emboldens the divide of the gap:

A bizarre permutation of the middle-class American ethos from which it evolved: they are predominantly white, middle-class, educated youths, ranging in age from 17 to 25 (though some as old as 50 can be spotted). Over-endowed with all the qualities that make their generation so engaging, per-

plexing and infuriating, they are dropouts from a way of life that, to them, seems wholly oriented toward work, status and power. They scorn money– they call it 'bread'– and property, and have found, like countless other romantics from Rimbaud to George Orwell, that it is not easy to starve.

Hippies preach altruism and mysticism, honesty, joy and non-violence. They find an almost childish fascination in beads, blossoms and bells, blinding strobe lights and ear-shattering music, exotic clothing and erotic slogans. Their professed aim is nothing less than the subversion of Western society by 'flower power' and force of example. Although that sounds like a pipe-dream, it conveys the unreality that permeates hippiedom, a cult whose mystique derives essentially from the influence of hallucinogenic drugs. Unlike other accepted stimuli, from nicotine to liquor, the hallucinogens promise those who take the "trip" a magic-carpet escape from reality in which perceptions are heightened, senses distorted, and the imagination permanently bedazzled with visions of teleological verity.

And we worry about generational angst of the 21st century! You really must be kidding!

SO TODAY, HERE IS THE ISSUE.

The Gen Xers, Millennials, Gen Zers and now the Alphas (again, the stratifying of our demographics into these group names) have a growing disdain for us "Hippie/Boomer self-indulgent old people." Yep, sorry to say it, Boomers. In their eyes, we are how we perceived our parents when we were young– the irony of ironies. The number of Americans over 65 has been projected to double between now and 2050, to almost 90 million, with the population of those over 85 expected to grow even faster:

from 5.8 million now to 19 million by 2050. Centenarians (those over a hundred years old) are estimated to increase tenfold.

Younger people are falling behind economically, with 32% of 18-29 year olds either unemployed or underemployed: working in a part-time job while looking for more gainful employment. In a Newsweek article by Joel Kotkin, they are labeled *Generation Screwed.* Entitlement programs are a heavy albatross on underemployed people.

The Pew research center notes that older generations were "beneficiaries of good timing," in everything from a strong economy to a long rise in housing prices.

Us older Americans (yes, we are getting older) have got to understand the facts: No generation has suffered as much economically as our younger generations (Gen X, Millennials and Gen Z). Through adversity grows opportunity, as I say on the talk show. How about "put up or shut up!" We have got to take this situation and lead the mind shift of the 21st century in redefining how we all expect to increase our QOL. If we Boomers do not grasp the severity of this issue and help our own situation, along with that of our children, we are going to have no one to blame but ourselves. Don't count on entitlements, rely on your knowledge and work ethic.

We were trendsetters as young people. Now, we need to step up and do it again, leading by example, and yes, putting up and stepping up.

With Boomers turning 67 at a rate of 10,000 per day, perhaps we need to reevaluate our existence and understand generativity. The possibility of living to 100 or more is much higher today than in the days of our parents. In that possibility lives what I refer to as our opportunity to once again make change and improve the world. It is our Boomers Rock mantra, go out and *Ignite Your Life* and live the *Maximized Quality of Life* you deserve.

We gotta step up, Boomers!

Starting a movement is in our blood, and our children and grandchildren could use our help. It's time to leverage our knowledge and build the next great society. Anyone who wants in is welcome!

The Boomers Rock train is loading up, "All Aboard!"

BE FLEXIBLE

By Bill Kost

Entrepreneurs have a great ability to create change, be flexible, build companies and cultivate the kind of work environment in which they want to work.

Tory Burch

Life is complicated and can sometimes not turn out how one would wish– that is why being flexible in how you live your life, how you approach events in your life and advice you receive that is different from your current path and thinking is critical to a life well lived.

Being flexible has shown up in the sport of golf that I have played for nearly 48 years. Some of the most fun was when I was in high school at Lansing Eastern. I was fortunate enough to make the varsity team as a sophomore and in my very first match at Groesbeck GC was able to tie the record for low round with a 70, 2 under par. The next two matches were disheartening as I couldn't find my game and shot 86 in both contests. This would not be the first time the game would break me and send me to analyzing what went wrong. My coach, Tom Penrod, provided the necessary guidance and showed me a method to plotting all my shots which gave me a visual of what to work on in my game to get back to scoring. So in this case, I stayed flexible to listening to advice and a new way of looking at my golf game that would help bring me back in true form. The rest of the season was a learning experience and was enjoyable with a great group of guys that would become my very best friends.

More 'being flexible' showed up for me when I attended MSU and was pursuing the grade point needed to get into the business college. Well, as I have told others, accounting classes did me in and I received that special letter from MSU telling me to find an alternative major or you're no longer enrolled at MSU. So with the help of my dad and a counselor, we found the major of Public Affairs Management and graduated in a little more than 4 years from MSU. My goal was to stay flexible in what my major could be after my initial business degree aspirations were dashed. But I knew in the end that getting a degree from MSU in anything and not looking for the perfect major was really the goal so I start experiencing life and figuring out the next steps.

I have witnessed at MSU in my role as an employer, that finding a perfect major freezes people and some even take a year off to figure things out (which I believe to be a big mistake). I was thinking of 'being flexible.' Get that degree as quickly as possible from this Top 100 university, and get me out in the world - because that is where real life feeds you opportunity and friendships that help guide and define your interests and pursuits through the positive law of attraction.

As mentioned before, golf has been ever present in my life and helped me 'be flexible' on how to advance my passion for it. While at MSU, I was a member of the Michigan State University golf team and enjoyed the role of student-athlete. I was honored to play for the green and white, but as a freshman you have more experienced golfers in front of you that you need to beat in order to get onto the starting five and qualify for a coveted varsity letter. I remember our hall fame coach, Bruce Fossum, telling us freshman to 'do our talking with our golf clubs,' meaning, don't expect favors to get you into the starting lineup, you need to deliver results with your golf clubs and through consistency in scoring you will get your shot. So being flexible in expectations is important in order to understand how you arrive at your destination in performance and understanding what it takes to be a Big Ten athlete. Each year, my golf game and experience level improved, through practice and observing the best golfers in the Big Ten and how they approached their golf games. Many good times ensued and I received a varsity letter and jacket my senior year!

One's faith is a personal matter and I believe that being open to new experiences and being flexible to where you feel you are being led in your faith makes all the difference. I have been a long time Lutheran and from a very young age I remember our family attending St. Paul Lutheran Church - not really a choice but simply what we did on Sunday as a family. For many years and into my early forties I attended services at University Lutheran Church just off campus at MSU. I finally got to a point that the services were not speaking to me. I was going through the motions, doing service projects and helping around the church in different roles. So I decided to listen to that small voice in my head and attend a much larger church. Trinity Church had a great word-of-mouth from other friends and fellow believers. I ended up loving the new church and the music and team teaching approach with impactful messages and made a shift to giving regular attendance a shot and see if this was the spot God wanted me to be. I am still at this church and feel this is where I need to be at this time in my life– only through 'being flexible' and listening to my inner yearnings would I have made this change that has influenced my life in many positive ways and will for the foreseeable future.

Another example on 'being flexible' is my current role at MSU as Associate Director of Retail Food Services. I was fortunate to join MSU as a temporary worker in 1988 hoping that the position would turn into a full-time job with benefits. Through hard work, I did receive a full-time position within the Concessions Department - which has the responsibility of setting up all the athletic events on campus. This was a really fun and enjoyable job as being around all the MSU sports was fun and my organizational skills made a big difference in our operations which was energizing. I was in a variety of positions within Concessions, working up to Assistant Manager through 19 years, when my boss was promoted unexpectedly. I was facing the role of Interim Concessions Manager, which I never thought would be an option. While I felt confident in this role, it was a time of uncertainty. I held this job for approximately 9 months before I was encouraged by my boss to apply for my current role. This role wasn't even on my radar and there were honest moments of inadequacy in the application and interview process for this role. I believe that my general attitude of 'being flexible,' along with the support I received from colleagues and friends and my belief in continuous professional growth helped me to be open to this opportunity which I was fortunate to attain 9 years ago.

Lastly, my current embrace of 'being flexible' is evident in my current adventure with my health and well-being. I am fortunate to have developed a friendship with Tom Matt that centered around exercising at the gym and engaging in simple conversation. Through many workout sessions, Tom started to share his passion for helping others in life, health, and post-retirement and this exposed me to the important topic of gut health and its impact on one's overall health and lifestyle. As a result, I have stepped out of the typical American diet and have been flexible in learning more about how our body works. I have developed a personal passion and ownership of a diet supplemented with super foods such as cod liver oil, chlorella/spirulina, turmeric/curcumin, and wheat grass, to name a few. If I hadn't been flexible to changes in how I approach my diet and approaching 60s/MiddleLiving, I don't think I would be as confident about the future and passion to help others be their best self!

In ending, I admonish you to be flexible and don't rule out anything that comes your way - we can all do more than we think, so open yourself to the possibilities in your life, and step through to success!

———

Be Flexible

BE SUPPORTIVE

By Thomas F. Matt

This is a true story of a journey that I hope can inspire many– women and men, boys and girls– to become more active in their lives.

There is this thing in life that can determine if you are focused enough to withstand adversity, downtimes and hardship. It's called grit.

What is grit, really? I believe it is a word that's been used to describe many things, but it actually is a very specific word with a very specific meaning. When things get hard, you push harder; when you fail, you get back up stronger; when you don't see results, you do not get dejected, but you continue to pound away day after day, after day, with relentlessness, steadiness, heart and passion. That, my friends, is grit!

This past year, really the beginning of the winter semester at Michigan State University, was a usual winter grind. Regularly going into the gym in January, you can typically expect pitch dark mornings and brutally cold temperatures, and it is rough. It certainly takes a special kind of person to consistently show up. January always brings the New Year's resolution crowd, so there will be a quite a few newbies trying to work into their new goals, build habits, strengthen the resolve and get into shape.

By the end of January most of them are gone, back to the comfort of their warm beds and sleeping in.

Most of those wannabes lacked grit. However, this past

year, there was a particular student who pressed on, solo and stone-faced, resolute in grinding. This girl had something. I watched from afar to see if she had what it took to hang.

After the lightweights had burned up their ill-planned goals and went back to their old habits and routines, I decided to see what was up with this kid. This loner who seemed to have something, maybe talent, perhaps guts, and even possibly the all-important grit. As this student worked on a pretty decent plank (a core strengthening move) I commented on it to her. I do not even remember the whole thing, something simple, the reaction was pretty much "leave me alone old dude," and I liked it. This girl just might have 'It', the all-important grit!

Continuing on through the winter, I saw this hard-ass kid sticking to the routine, actually making progress, working a pretty solid routine of lifting and High Intensity Interval Training– pretty impressive actually. I really was starting to admire this girl's determination and grit, but I still thought she would fade away like so many before her, the delicate flower, wilting. I have seen this a thousand times. She, however, did not.

I made another comment to this girl. Typically, as a CPT (certified personal trainer), we are taught not to offer unsolicited advice to gym participants, but I had to know what this kid's game was. Usually a pretty active high-school athletic career is the norm. Virtually everyone I have ever met at the gym, especially the early morning warriors, has competed in something at the varsity or even club level. I would venture it's probably 99%. When I asked this young woman what her game was, her history, her sport, she said she did not do anything, nothing! She read books! Read books? Come on, no way!

If you ever doubt yourself, if you ever think you can't fit in, use my friend's example of a journey into the lion's den: a place which can sometimes be compared to the college gym facility. The home where young warriors live, not welcoming the novice or bookworm newbie with no experience.

That is, until you read this testimonial and it changes your mind:

A year ago, I was a very insecure and unhealthy person. I thought the solution was to go without food and sprint myself away. I had very little mobility and even less strength, and I was simply miserable all the time. Now, I'm still a string bean, but instead of working to eliminate myself I get up every day to make myself stronger. I'm the heaviest I've ever been, but I'm also the strongest, most capable, and happiest I've ever been. It's uncomfortable, and sometimes seems nearly impossible, but I promise this fitness stuff is all it's cracked up to be and more. – Samantha Medved

The hardest part of change is always the first step. Do not let a fear or lack of perceived talent dissuade your effort. People see talent, but what they fail to see is the work behind accomplishments, the grit, the grinding, the loneliness and the anxiety. We all go through it; you are not alone. The idea of 'God-given talent' gives someone an out, an excuse, if you think about it. You were not blessed with incredible once-in-a-generation skills, so you get a pass for not achieving success as an athlete, fit person or participant of life. What most of us do not see behind the talented, strong person: those who become massive success stories in their own right; is a daily schedule of grind, hours of sucking it up and a whole regimen of difficult, and sometimes lonely, moments when the only partner you have is the music playing in your head. It is the tiniest of details, it is the desire to find yourself and it is your inner grit that can drive you.

Use my friend Samantha's story as a catalyst. She had no game, no experience, no training; that is, until she walked through the door on a cold January morning. Alone and stone-faced, she sucked it up, and now you know the story!

——

Be Supportive

I LOVE LUCY

By Thomas F. Matt

---

the QUIETER you become, the more you are able to HEAR.
-Rumi

One of the things I learned the hard way was that it doesn't pay to get discouraged. Keeping busy and making optimism a way of life can restore your faith in yourself.
Lucille Ball

I Love Lucy is definitely in my top three favorite television programs of all time. The sitcom, starring Lucille Ball and Desi Arnaz as husband and wife, with Vivian Vance and William Frawley as the landlords of their apartment, was such a classic. There were so many great memories of Lucy and her zany antics; she was the epitome of funny. Her physical humor was a leader in craziness. She was the best!

Visits to our grandparents' house enabled us to watch these syndicated reruns, and even though they were obviously repeats, who cared? Not us, that was for sure. All of these early TV classics were outstanding, and since we rarely had access to them, it made our visits even better. Think about that: how many kids of the 21st century look forward to traveling to the grandparents' house for the weekend, sometimes even a whole week, in the summer to watch '40s and '50s television classics? Probably about zero!

In 2002, *I Love Lucy* was ranked second on TV Guide's list of television's greatest shows, behind *Seinfeld* and ahead of *The Honeymooners*. In 2007, it was listed as one of Time magazine's *100 Best TV Shows of All-Time*. They would have gotten my vote if anyone had asked.

I Love Lucy was the first scripted television program to be shot on 35mm film in front of a live studio audience, which at this point in history was a major change. It was through these technological challenges that would inadvertently lead to the creation of 'Desilu' productions, and set in stone the star and business power of Lucille Ball and Desi Arnaz (more on this later as an interesting side note, because as you know I am all about discovering the tech stuff behind the scenes). All of the technological and foundational building blocks that brought us to where we are now are important. The *I Love Lucy* show was a pioneer in more ways than one, that is for certain.

I Love Lucy was the most-watched show in the United States in four of its six seasons, and was the first to end its run at the top of the Nielsen ratings (an accomplishment later matched by *The Andy Griffith Show* and *Seinfeld*). *I Love Lucy* is still syndicated in dozens of languages around the world. *I Love Lucy* won five Emmy Awards and received numerous nominations. I am one to admit that the episode in 1952, where Lucy tries through the whole half hour show to tell Ricky they were going to have a baby, was completely awesome. I remember how Ricky was passed a note describing a woman who was trying to tell her husband the great news, and unbeknownst to him, Ricky was the father. He notices Lucy in the audience, and it occurs to him that Lucy may be the one who is expecting. Lucy nods yes, and Ricky is overcome with emotion. They fight happy tears and sing *We're Having a Baby.* It brings a happy memory to me just thinking about it. If you never saw this, it is worth the effort to try and find.

The black-and-white original series would run from October 15, 1951 to May 6, 1957 on CBS. However, after the series ended in 1957, a modified version continued for three more seasons with 13 one-hour specials, running from 1957 to 1960. It was known first as *The Lucille Ball-Desi Arnaz Show* and later in reruns as *The Lucy-Desi Comedy Hour.* It really did not matter to me which of the 'Lucy' shows I watched as a kid, syndication gave us the full 181 original episodes, and later in the '60s *The Lucy Show.*

EARLY LUCY

Loving Lucy was easy. I mean, she was so darned talented as a kid, how could you not like her? Much like Lucille Ball herself, Lucy McGillicuddy was born and raised in Jamestown, New York (or West Jamestown per episode #138), on August 6th, 1911 to an American family of Scottish descent. Her parents were never referred to by name, and only her mother is seen over the course of the series, portrayed by Kathryn Card. As a child, she was babysat by Helen Kaiser, who gave her the nickname 'Droopy Drawers' because of her baggy bloomers.

Lucille Ball had come to Hollywood in 1933 when, after a successful stint as a New York model, she was chosen by Sam Goldwyn to be one of sixteen Goldwyn Girls to co-star in the film *Roman Scandals* with Eddie Cantor. As with most of our stars of television, where Lucy would eventually become a household name, film was her intro in becoming noticed.

Animated and hard-working, Lucy had been able to secure film work fleetingly at the Samuel Goldwyn Studio and Columbia Pictures, and then eventually at RKO Radio Pictures. It was at RKO that Ball received steady film work, first as an extra and bit player, eventually working her way up to co-starring roles in feature films and starring roles in second-rate B pictures, collectively earning the nickname 'Queen of the B's.' During her run at RKO, Ball gained the reputation for doing physical comedy and stunts that most other actresses avoided, keeping her steadily employed.

In 1940, Lucy met Desi Arnaz, a Cuban bandleader who had just come off a successful run in the 1939-40 Broadway show *Too Many Girls.* RKO had bought the film rights to the show and cast Ball as Arnaz's love interest in the picture. The duo began a whirlwind courtship leading to their elopement to Connecticut in November 1940. Despite being madly in love, however, their careers kept them separated, with Lucy's film work keeping her anchored in Hollywood, while Desi's nightclub engagements with his orchestra kept him on the road.

To me, Lucy was the consummate pioneer of an early sort of aggressive female mentality. She worked extremely hard at her craft, made sure her ambitions matched her family and she just went for it. This had to be hard, because in the '40s and '50s, women were in the midst of a changing world: working outside the home, wanting more for their families and wanting more in their personal lives. Like everything else, the times were changing.

The early days of the *I Love Lucy* show were fraught with issues, some of which go back to what I stated earlier about the way the show was filmed. Like most of the early television programming, TV content was produced in front of a live audience and recorded. For the bulk of the content being created, television shows were produced from New York with live broadcasts airing for Eastern and Midwest audiences. West Coast viewers were able to view recorded live programs only through low-quality kinescopes, which derived their images by using a 35mm or 16mm film camera to record the show off a closed-circuit television monitor. Videotape had not yet been developed, and would not be until the mid-fifties, so kinescopes were the only practical and affordable means to allow a live show to reach television markets on the West coast. Complicating matters was the fact that kinescopes were not available for immediate re-broadcast. In 1951, there was no coast-to-coast network of cables (telephone or coaxial cable) and, of course, satellites were a dream for the next decade. Television shows had to be physically shipped to the West coast, if the show had been recorded in New York, or vice versa. It must have seemed like the 'Pony Express' delivering the mail, plus the Interstate Highway system was still on the drawing board. You had to be patient.

With the impending birth of their first child in 1951, both

Lucy and Desi Arnaz insisted on staying in Hollywood and producing the *I Love Lucy* show on film, something few Hollywood-based series had begun doing. Both the network, CBS, and the sponsor, Philip Morris, initially hesitated at the idea. Their reasoning was due to the greater costs the show would incur. They agreed, but only after the pair offered to take a one-thousand-dollar a week pay cut in order to cover the additional expense. This would give Lucy and Desi the majority ownership in the *I Love Lucy* films, which they demanded if they were to pay the extra cost. In the long run, this proved to be quite the astute move.

Recording the show on film required Lucy and Desi to become responsible for producing the series themselves. Union contracts at the time required that any production filmed in a studio use film studio employees. CBS staffs were television and radio employees and fell under different union agreements. Thus, Arnaz reorganized the company he created to manage his orchestra bookings and used it as the corporation that would produce the *I Love Lucy* show. Named after their ranch in Chatsworth, California, the company was called Desilu.

Jess Oppenheimer was the series creator, producer and head writer for the first five years of production. Lucille Ball called him "the brains behind the *I Love Lucy* show." It was reported that Lucille Ball herself insisted that Oppenheimer head up the new show, and he did. Oppenheimer decided that Lucy needed to perform in front of a live audience to create the kind of comic energy she had exhibited on radio. Lucy and her comic energy transference to television would not have occurred if Oppenheimer had not run the show.

The idea of a film studio (remember that for the most part of the early TV days, these studios were in New York) that could accommodate an audience was a new one for the time, and fire laws made it difficult to allow an audience in a studio. Desi Arnaz and Oppenheimer were fortunate enough to find the financially-struggling General Service Studios located on Las Palmas Avenue in Hollywood. Studio owner Jimmy Nasser was eager to accommodate and allowed them, with the financial backing of CBS, to renovate two of his studios so that they could host an audience and be in compliance with local fire laws.

Though some television series were already being filmed in Hollywood, most used the single-camera format familiar to movies, with a laugh track added to comedies to simulate audience response. This would change with *I Love Lucy* (another pioneering move that would carry over into the future of television sitcoms) with the introduction of the three-camera design. It was decided by Oppenheimer to use three 35mm film cameras to simultaneously film the show.

The idea had been pioneered by Ralph Edwards on the game show *Truth or Consequences*. Edwards's assistant, Al Simon, was hired by Desilu to help perfect the new method for the series. The process lent itself to the *Lucy* production as it eliminated the problem of requiring an audience to view and react to a scene three or four times in order for all necessary shots to be filmed. Multiple cameras would also allow scenes to be performed in sequence, as a play would be, which was uncommon at the time for filmed series. Retakes were rare and dialogue mistakes were often played off for the sake of continuity. In addition, audience reactions were live, thus creating a far more authentic laugh than the 'canned laughter' used on most filmed sitcoms of the time. Regular audience members were sometimes heard from episode to episode, and Arnaz's characteristic laugh could be heard in the background during scenes in which he did not perform. I believe that goes to show how much fun the crew would have and how genuinely funny Lucy was. It was comedy at its best and it helped build my sense of humor as I am sure it did for many people of the '50s, '60s and beyond. It was a true gift to have grown up having *I Love Lucy*.

BE FUN

By Thomas F. Matt

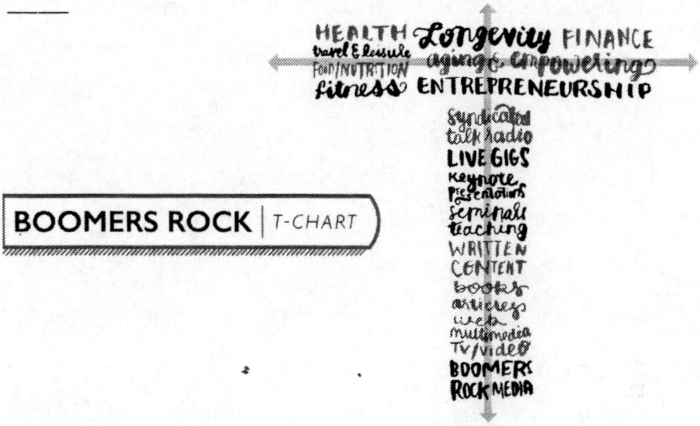

BOOMERS ROCK | T-CHART

Fun is one of the most important– and underrated– ingredients in any successful venture. If you're not having fun, then it's probably time to call it quits and try something else.
Richard Branson

Is there a difference between being fun and having fun?

Generationally speaking, probably not. In a strictly grammatical sense, yes, there is a big difference. In the timelines defined within generations, being fun stays pretty constant. If you are fun to be around, it does not matter if you are 90 or 20, being fun at any age is cool. Not being fun is, well, not so cool. I have always wanted to be around fun people, those who are different, those who may have vastly different cultures, those who are of opposite sexes, it did not matter. Being fun, and surrounding yourself with like-minded souls makes for a good time.

Having fun– now that can be a vastly different perspective

and paradigm, funky, yes, for sure owned by each. Where perspective is a funny paradox of beliefs that exist in what we call the 'generational divide,' the one that this book is trying to dissuade everyone from perpetuating, could come down to this simple thing. If we can understand each other's level of fun, what it is, how we do it, where we go, and how we embrace it; then the understanding that makes us all human comes clearly into focus.

I was a pinball kid, loved it, and still would like to have a machine in my house. Those silver balls rolling down the board, the flippers sometimes working and sometimes not, made for a game that was a great time-sucker for the younger Boomer youth. Clicking, clacking, bells, lights and of course quarters, lots and lots of quarters. As a paper boy, I spent a lot of hard earned paper delivery money on clicking and clacking, flippers and tilting.

I loved outdoor team sports. We did not have much money, but it didn't take much to get kids together and throw a football around or play baseball in our backyard. We played touch football in the street. The curbs were the out-of-bounds markers and getting tackled happened occasionally. Street lights served as iPhone alarms; when they came on, we better be heading inside.

As we aged a bit, we roamed the neighborhood at night. Yes, there were the tenuous moments of getting into the youthful trouble, ring and run, minor vandalism, simple stuff but never anything that caused damage. We ran and we played and we rode bikes and we built forts and we played army.

The pros of having fun like that are nearly countless. Having fun brings people together. It makes you smile/laugh. It can sometimes mean that you are on a roller coaster or that you're having a birthday. Having fun makes you laugh a lot. It diverts your attention from dark truths in the world. It is the best.

Meanwhile, there are literally no cons to having fun. You could try for an hour and you wouldn't be able to think of one, which makes the reality that we sometimes don't have fun all the more perplexing.

Honestly, life will not always be fun. Maybe a loved one is in the hospital, or you will have to help someone struggling with the basics of life. Fun, however, does not disappear. It can be in the background waiting to take away the hard times. Just keep in mind that fun is what we decide to be fun. It can be a simple visit with a friend over coffee. Life is forever challenging, but staying willing to accept the fun moments as they are presented can help you persevere.

When is the last time you really had fun? Think about it–the last time you just let yourself go and had a good time? When did you last forget about all your daily responsibilities and live in the moment? If it's been too long, one of these assumptions about fun may be holding you back:

1. YOU'RE WORRIED WHAT OTHER PEOPLE WILL THINK.

You don't want to look silly in front of other people. You're afraid they'll judge you. Guess what? Other people don't think about you nearly as much as you think they do. Besides, you're not a mind reader. You don't know what is going on in other people's minds. And if they are judging you for being silly and having a good time, then they're people you don't need to know anyway. To quote Dr. Seuss: "Be who you are and say what you feel, because those who mind don't matter and those who matter don't mind."

2.
YOU THINK YOU NEED TO SPEND MONEY.

It's true: Some of the best things in life are free. You don't need to go on a pricey vacation or buy a lot of stuff to have fun. Many times it's just being in the moment with the people you care about. And that costs nothing. Check newspaper listings or your town's website for ideas of fun low-cost activities in your community.

3.
YOU THINK YOU DON'T HAVE THE TIME.

There is always time to have fun. I don't care who you are or how little time you think you have– you can make the time. Also, fun is found in the little moments– you don't need to carve out your whole day. Block out a half-hour to do something you enjoy, just for the fun of it.

4.
YOU THINK YOU NEED TO PLAN IT.

If you're a Type A planner, keep in mind that the most fun can be found in spontaneous unplanned moments. Let things happen naturally. Let yourself experience spur-of-the-moment trips and last-minute get-togethers. Be in the present moment.

5. YOU MISTAKE SOLEMNITY FOR SERIOUSNESS.

As Jim Morrison wrote, "No one gets out of here alive." You've got one life, and it's short. Enjoy it. It is possible to take something seriously and still inject some fun and humor into it. For example, if you've ever flown Southwest Airlines, you've seen how the company takes something serious, like safety instructions, and turns it into something fun. By doing this, not only will people enjoy themselves more, they're also more likely to pay attention. So whoop it up at your next staff meeting. (Just don't tell your boss I recommended that.)

6. YOU THINK CONDITIONS HAVE TO BE PERFECT.

Many fun moments occur when things go unexpectedly awry. Allow yourself to be imperfect, and to enjoy the imperfections of life. Humans are imperfect creatures, after all, and you're one of them. Telling yourself, "I'll have fun when…" is counterproductive and, frankly, a real bummer. Have fun now– there's no time like the present.

7. YOU THINK IT HAS TO BE BIG AND SPECTACULAR.

News flash: Every day is not 4th of July fireworks, parades and parties. You can find fun in small moments. If you think real fun only happens at big events, you're depriving yourself of some good times. Fun is what you make it. It doesn't need to be spectacular, by any means. Sometimes it's found in 5- and 10-minute increments.

8.
YOU'RE BORED.

There's a symptom of depression called anhedonia, in which you no longer find interest or fun in things that previously got you excited. Also, with ADHD, it can be difficult to keep up novel tasks to excite the brain. On the other hand, if you're just plain bored, that is a choice. You make the changes and opportunities in your life.

GET OUT THERE AND HAVE FUN

- Be amusing and joke around
- Introduce people to fun new activities and situations
- Help people have more fun than they normally do themselves
- Get in touch with your goofy, immature side
- Be a little more crazy and reckless than you would normally
- Take things a little further than you normally would
- Have tricks and talents that make you more fun

BEING LESS 'UN-FUN'

- Don't be the person who never wants to do anything
- Wherever you are, don't just hang back and do nothing
- Don't be too picky about what you require to be entertained

A person hanging back at the party while their friends are

off elsewhere could just be shy or not know what to say to people, it's hard to tell.

While the less-fun people are making a tally of what's wrong with the place, their more-fun friends are out there dancing, meeting people, talking and having a good time.

- Make the best of whatever situation you're in. Focus on the positives instead of the negatives.
- Don't feel you can only have fun under the perfect circumstances.
- Don't sit back and wait for the amusement to come to you
- Don't be a downer
- Don't be overly serious

Being too uptight can generally contribute to people being less fun. As I wrote earlier, having fun often involves letting loose and acting less proper and controlled than you normally do. Lighten up a little. You can't bring rigid, serious, humorless sensibilities to fun situations.

Don't see having fun as immature or beneath you!

Be Fun

LEAVE IT TO BEAVER

By Thomas F. Matt

Where would my memories and comedy of my mind be without 'the Beaver?' Jerry Mathers would be a kid that, much like myself, was always in a state of wonderment. I kinda wished I had an older brother like him. Tony Dow would play 'Wally' and mom and dad, played by Barbara Billingsley and Hugh Beaumont, were the consummate American family of the '50s as the Beaver's parents. They all lived in that perfect American middle class city of Mayfield.

As another one of the television shows that would be viewed through syndication, where most of the early '50s programming would originate, reruns were actually first runs for me. 'The Beave' was like my TV brother and extra part of my life.

Leave it to Beaver would attain iconic status in American television history, having a run of six seasons and 234 episodes. It first aired on CBS television October 4, 1957. The following year *Beaver* would move to ABC, completing its run on June 20, 1963. The popular show was canceled in 1963 because the stars wanted to move on. Jerry Mathers was entering his freshman year in high school (hard to imagine The Beaver in high school) and actor Tony Dow was about to graduate from high school.

One of the first primetime sitcom series written from a child's point-of-view, the show was created by writers Joe Connelly and Bob Mosher. These veterans of radio and early television found inspiration for the show's characters, plots and dialogue in the lives, experiences and conversations of their own children. *Leave It to Beaver* was a look into middle-class, white American boyhood. In a classic episode, Beaver got into some kind of distress, (didn't we all have similar issues?) and then faced the music from his parents for lectures and correction. However, neither parent was well-informed. A classic trait of this show was showing that parents could be clueless, and many of the episodes were built around parental blunders. It is what would endear *Leave it to Beaver* to me, the growing up and having parents that were not all that sure of themselves.

As I grew up, I clearly remember referring to friends who would suck up to parents as being 'Eddie Haskell,' a role that fit actor Ken Osmond as he perfected the "Gee, Mrs. Cleaver, your hair sure looks pretty today!" I'm sure many of us remember how Eddie was a pain to our boy, The Beaver.

The star of the show was, of course, Jerry Mathers as Theodore "The Beaver" Cleaver. As I grew up watching the syndicated versions of the TV show, I completely identified with the dark-haired, freckle-faced kid– I'm sure millions of other boys did as well. Mathers was born in 1948 in Sioux City, Iowa, the son of a high school principal. He has two younger siblings, Susie and Jim Mathers, who also became child actors. He began his career at the age of 2 when he performed as a child model for a department store ad. Soon after, he starred in a commercial for PET Milk, opposite vaudeville comedian Ed Wynn. His early movies included *This is My Love* (1954), *Men of the Fighting Lady* (1954), *The Seven Little Foys* (1955) and *The Trouble with Harry* (1955).

Jerry Mathers has been in show business for most of his life.

Mathers reportedly got the role of Beaver Cleaver when he told the show's producers he would rather be at his Cub Scout meeting than be auditioning for the part. Sounds like something a regular kid would say. I mean, frankly, at nine years old, how many kids would rather work than go to a Cub Scout meeting? The producers of the show reportedly found his honesty appealing and perfect for the role. Jerry Mathers would play The Beaver for six years, appearing in all 234 episodes of the series.

Jerry Mathers would give up his role just before his freshman year in high school. He attended Notre Dame High school in Sherman Oaks, California, and went on to attend college at Cal Berkley. Mathers graduated with a Bachelor of Arts degree in philosophy in 1973. He then worked at a bank as a commercial loan officer until he used his well-invested savings from acting (which began at $500 a week) to begin a career in real-estate development. It was reported that Jerry Mathers was one of the first child actors to get a percentage of his merchandising revenue– a very smart move on his part.

In 1978, he reentered the entertainment industry. That year, he and Tony Dow starred in the play *Boeing, Boeing* which ran for ten weeks in Kansas City. Mathers and Dow then toured the dinner theater circuit in a production of *So Long, Stanley* for 18 months. In 1981, he worked as a disc jockey at KEZY-AM radio in Anaheim, California. In 1983, Mathers reenacted his role in the 1983 television reunion film *Still the Beaver,* which also featured the majority of the original *Leave It to Beaver* cast. The triumph of the small screen film lead to the development of a sequel series of the same name which began airing on the Disney Channel in 1984. It went on to be picked up by TBS and broadcast syndication, where it was retitled *The New Leave It to Beaver* and ran until 1989.

Mathers has since sustained his profession in films and television roles. In the 1990s, he guest starred on episodes of *Parker Lewis Can't Lose, Vengeance Unlimited* and *Diagnosis: Murder.* In 1998, Mathers released his memoir, *And Jerry Mathers as The Beaver.* On June 5, 2007, he made his Broadway debut with a starring role as Wilbur Turnblad in the Tony-winning best musical *Hairspray* at the Neil Simon Theater.

In addition to acting, Mathers has also owned and operated a catering business and has done national and regional commercials for companies such as PET Condensed Milk, Kellogg's (he and Tony Dow were the first non-athletes on a box of Corn Flakes), General Electric, Purina, Kern International, Chevrolet, Toyota, General Mills, AOL, Coca Cola, Jim Beam and Biogen.

In 2009, Mathers became the national spokesman for PhRMA and their Partnership for Prescription Assistance program. The organization helps uninsured and financially struggling patients obtain prescription medicines. Mathers was diagnosed with Type 2 diabetes in 1996. On the advice of his doctor, Mathers enrolled in a weight loss program with Jenny Craig in May 1997 and lost over 40 pounds. He later became the first male spokesperson for Jenny Craig.

Mathers has been married three times. He met his first wife, Diana Piatt, in college. They married in 1974 and divorced six years later. Mathers met his second wife, Rhonda Gehring, while touring in the production of *So Long, Stanley.* They have three children: two sons and a daughter. Mathers and Gehring later divorced. Mathers married his third wife, Teresa Modnick, in Huntington Beach on January 30th, 2011.

All-in-all one of my favorite shows, *Leave it to Beaver* was highly regarded. Current reporters praised *Leave it to Beaver*, with Variety likening *Beaver* to Mark Twain's *Tom Sawyer.* TV Land celebrated *Beaver* by acknowledging the 50th anniversary with a marathon. Heady stuff to be sure, and even though the show never cracked into the Nielsen Top 30 nor won any awards, it placed on Time Magazine's 2007 unranked list of 'The 100 Best TV Shows of All-Time.'

Leave it to Beaver is an American classic. Its longevity and popularity are obvious; it brings back memories of many Baby Boomers' childhoods. It was and still is great American television content, and one of my all-time favorites even today.

NOTE

In 1998, when I was in the darkest stretches of overcoming and dealing with my drinking issues, my therapist Dr. Pat Long helped me to understand how my mind worked. He used the '50s style mentality' analogy when describing how I thought. This was very helpful in my burgeoning sobriety. Looking back almost twenty years later, I know that this thinking had its roots in this television program. It is one reason that I wanted to include this television show in my book. Thank you Jerry Mathers and the creators of Leave it to Beaver.

REFERENCES

en.wikipedia.org/wiki/Jerry_Mathers

www.imdb.com/character/ch0036409/quotes

en.wikipedia.org/wiki/Leave_It_to_Beaver

www.leaveittobeaver.org

JACKIE GLEASON

By Thomas F. Matt

How sweet it was, (ok...a take-off on the classic Gleason line *'How Sweet it Is'*) Jackie Gleason was a complete character and beloved in our home. My dad enjoyed watching us kids bust a gut laughing at all of Jackie Gleason's hilarity. Gleason was an extremely talented guy who could make you die laughing and then switch gears into a more dramatic role. He had a very interesting life. Ralph Kramden will always be part of my fondest memories.

John Herbert Gleason, (February 26, 1916 – June 24, 1987) known professionally as Jackie Gleason, was an American comedian, actor and musician. He was known for his impetuous visual and verbal comedy style, exemplified by his character Ralph Kramden in *The Honeymooners.* Among his notable film roles were Minnesota Fats in the 1961 drama *The Hustler* (starring Paul Newman) and Buford T. Justice in the *Smokey and the Bandit* series. From the *Jackie Gleason Show,* which was the precursor to the famed *Honeymooners,* to his role as Minnesota Fats or Burt Reynolds' nemesis in the *Smokey* series of films, Jackie Gleason rocked, and is in my hall of fame. As with many of the future celebrity stars, Gleason had modest beginnings.

As a young man, reportedly aged 24, Jackie Gleason was acting in movies: first for Warner Brothers (as Jackie C. Gleason) in such films as *Navy Blues* (1941) with Ann Sheridan and Martha Raye, and *All Through the Night* (1941) with Humphrey Bogart; for Columbia Pictures' B military comedy *Tramp, Tramp, Tramp* (1942); and finally for Twentieth Century-Fox, where Gleason played Glenn

Miller Orchestra bassist Ben Beck in *Orchestra Wives* (1942). He also had a small part as a soda shop clerk in *Larceny, Inc.* (1942) with Edward G. Robinson, and a modest part as a commissioner in the 1942 Betty Grable/Harry James musical *Springtime in the Rockies.* He really was not making a breakthrough into the inner circles of Hollywood. It would be his raucous stand-up comedian days of the late '40s that would launch his career into the world of small-screen television and super-stardom. Jackie Gleason was the early version of another wild man, John Belushi, who had his hotel rooms soundproofed because of his loud partying. Many thought he would never amount to much. Those people never saw the explosion of TV in the fifties coming, when acts like Gleason blew up the small screen. I, for one, am glad the critics were wrong.

Gleason's nightclub act had received attention from New York City's inner circle and the untried DuMont Television Network. Gleason worked at Slapsy Maxie's when he was hired to host DuMont's *Cavalcade of Stars* variety hour in 1950.

The program initially had rotating hosts, and the offer first made to Gleason was for two weeks at $750 per week. When he said he did not consider that worth the train trip to New York, the offer was extended to four weeks. Gleason then returned to New York. He framed the show with splashy dance numbers, developed sketch characters which he would refine over the next decade, and became enough of a presence that CBS wooed (and won) him over to its network in 1952.

Renamed *The Jackie Gleason Show,* it became the country's second-highest-rated television show during the 1954-1955 season. Gleason amplified the show with even splashier opening dance numbers, inspired by Busby Berkeley screen dance routines and featuring the precision-choreographed June Taylor Dancers. Following the dance performance, he would do an opening monologue. Then, accompanied by "a little travelin' music," (*That's a Plenty*, a Dixieland classic from 1914) he would shuffle toward the wings, clapping his hands inversely and shouting, "And awaaay we go!" The phrase became one of his trademarks, along with "How sweet it is!" (which was used in reaction to almost anything). This show was the lead in to Gleason's fame as Ralph Kramden and *The Honeymooners.*

The Honeymooners made its debut as a half-hour series on October 1, 1955. Although initially a ratings success, becoming the #2 show in the United States its first season, it faced stiff competition from the *Perry Como Show* and eventually dropped to #19, ending its production after only 39 episodes. During that time, with the cast of Art Karney (Ed Norton) and his wife Alice (Audrey Meadows), the legacy was built and technology proved innovative. The shows were filmed with a new DuMont process Electronicam which captured a live performance on film but with higher quality comparable to a motion picture. That turned out to be the most perceptive move Gleason made, because a decade afterward, those half-hour shows aired in syndication through reruns. The Honeymooners began to build a loyal and growing audience, including my family, who made the show a television icon. Reportedly, the syndication success brought the 39 episodes, combined with the *Jackie Gleason Show*, up to over 100 episodes. Like much of the early video content of the 20th century, syndication and re-purposing would be extremely profitable and entertaining to a whole new generation.

The Honeymooners' popularity was such that a life-size statue of Jackie Gleason, in uniform as bus driver Ralph Kramden, stands outside the Port Authority Bus Terminal in New York City.

The final episode of *The Honeymooners* aired on September 22, 1956. Hard to believe!

REFERENCES

en.wikipedia.org/wiki/Jackie_Gleason

en.wikipedia.org/wiki/100_episodes

classic-tv.com/50s-shows/

THE SIXTIES AND TV

By Thomas F. Matt

Things really started to change in the '60s as far as our television content. All of the improvements that were developed on the technological side of things, such as better cameras and the three-camera studio developed by Desilu, made content better. However, the transmission of programming (remember, there was no cross country telephone service, satellites or the internet) made simultaneous broadcasts impossible for all time zones. Everything was quickly improving as far as technology was concerned. This made for better quality content, which in turn led to us running home from school or setting up special evenings as a family to watch our shows.

Hello Gilligan, hello Fred Munster!

Many of the shows that I personally watched were now a combination of repeated syndication of our earlier 1950s shows and now the networks were getting serious about new and improved content. And color was just around the corner: another step forward in our in home viewing. From 1960-69, there were so many great new shows. I am sure that this list will not be complete, and frankly that is the fun of all of this, because I look forward to feedback from you on your families' happy times and viewing habits.

As time would tell, the backwoods, lowbrow, as some writers claimed, type of shows were very popular in the 1960s. Many favorites of mine (and I am sure yours as well) had a family in a rural themed genre. As you will see in my top five, these comedies were classics of a time gone by. I believe it is why they are still loved now, some fifty plus years later. The hipper, more urbanized television programming would take hold in the seventies as the mood shifted, but the sixties were a transition from the fifties that blended well. It just seems like it was a smooth handoff; from my favorites like *Lucy* to Andy Taylor, Uncle Jed, and Mr. Douglas; you can probably tell where we are going with this. Dubbed 'ruralcoms,' the '60s proved to the world that television, slapstick and take-off humor would work. We were moving from a physical comedy into more of a situation comedy, where the shows appealed to children through its slapstick, silliness, shtick and goofiness, and adults were able to appreciate it on their level. The writing and story lines were improving.

Keep in mind that, due to the amount of content that television was producing, and how influential I feel comedy is in my becoming what I am today, that other genres of television programming will be coming in later books. I would love input on what you would like to see: westerns, dramas, cop shows, daytime soaps or thrillers. I was allowed to watch as much TV as I could, so I have my feelings for specific genres, and I'm sure you do, too.

THE ANDY GRIFFITH SHOW
1960-1968, 249 EPISODES

This show was definitely a TV classic. Andy (Andy Griffith), the main character, was a widowed sheriff fathering a boy named Opie (Ron Howard). Identifying with Opie was simple for us boys. He really was just like us– kind of a cross between Theodore Cleaver (Beaver) and Dennis Mitchell (The Menace). Opie Taylor was a little bit younger when this show started, six years old, and he was being raised in what would be labeled a single-parent household in today's world.

The title sequence showed Andy walking hand-in hand with Opie, going to the fishing hole. That was the name of the show's theme song: "The Fishin' Hole," composed by Earle Hagen and Herbert Spencer, with lyrics written by Everett Sloane. It was writer Earle Hagen who was doin' the whislin' (sorry for the misspelling, but it is in respect for the show, bringing back memories as I write). Aunt Bee (Frances Bavier) was the very loving and caring, but also stern & old-fashioned, housekeeper for Andy and Opie. Aunt Bee was always giving out her advice to the single dad Andy; she was an integral part of the whole family dynamic. Many times she was the buffer for the two guys in the house and all Sheriff Taylor's issues.

Local well-meaning friends, bumbling pals and temperamental girlfriends further complicate Sheriff Taylor's life. Andy Griffith stated in a Today Show interview, with respect to the time period of the show, "Well, though we never said it, and though it was shot in the '60s, it had a feeling of the '30s. It was when we were doing it, of a time gone by." It was this mentality that made this such a classic.

Andy Taylor worked with anxious, nervous, jumpy and very suspicious Barney Fife, played by Don Knotts. ("Nip-it. Nip-it in the bud!") They all lived in the nice southern town of Mayberry, North Carolina. But, Mayberry can get a little dangerous when the town drunk Otis Campbell (Hal Smith) is on the loose. Thelma Lou (Betty Lynn) is

Barney's sweetheart, although Andy had to help him describe his feelings to her. Gomer Pyle (Jim Nabors) is the bone-headed and thoughtless, but humorous character. He is a gas attendant. Goober Pyle (George Lindsey) is Gomer Pyle's cousin. They are very alike, you could say, and he arrives in Mayberry when Gomer decides to enlist in the United States Marine Corps. The show had two spin-offs: *Gomer Pyle U.S.M.C.* and *Mayberry R.F.D.*

The show was a spin-off from an episode of *The Danny Thomas Show* titled "Danny Meets Andy Griffith," which aired on February 15th, 1960. In the episode, Griffith played Sheriff Taylor of Mayberry, North Carolina, and arrested Danny Williams (Thomas's character) for running a stop sign. The future cast of *The Andy Griffith Show* would start here, as Frances Bavier and Ron Howard appeared in the episode as townspeople Henrietta Perkins and Opie Taylor (the sheriff's son). The blending of radio and film stars continued to build on the popularity of the small screen, giving us the classics that we're still watching today.

REFERENCES

www.tv.com/shows/the-andy-griffith-show/

en.wikipedia.org/wiki/The_Andy_Griffith_Show

en.wikipedia.org/wiki/Green_Acres

THE BEVERLY HILLBILLIES

By Thomas F. Matt

Come and listen to a story about a man named Jed...
From the Ballad of Jed Clampett by Paul Henning

That theme song reached an unbelievable number one on the country charts in 1962, and number 44 in the overall billboard as well. It's an American culture classic!

"We-e-e-ell, doggies!"

The Beverly Hillbillies was an American situation comedy originally broadcast for nine seasons on CBS from 1962 to 1971, starring Buddy Ebsen (Uncle Jed), Irene Ryan (Granny), Donna Douglas (Ellie Mae) and Max Baer Jr. (Jethro).

The Beverly Hillbillies ranked among the top twenty most-watched programs on television for eight of its nine seasons, twice ranking as the number one series of the year. A number of episodes remain among the most-watched television episodes of all time. For the first two seasons, 1962 & 1963, it was the back-to-back number one show on television!

After selling his swamp to the OK Oil Company for $25 million, Cousin Pearl convinces Jed he should move his family to Beverly Hills. So Jed, along with his gorgeous daughter Elly May, feisty mother-in-law Granny and half-witted nephew Jethro, all head to this new land inhabited by movie stars and the well-off.

Jed and his family get to Beverly Hills, and their money

goes into the Commerce Bank of Beverly Hills, with President Milburn Drysdale. Jane Hathaway, the secretary to Mr. Drysdale, always had a serious crush on Jethro. Man that must have been tough on her!

For the nine years the clan is in Beverly Hills, all kinds of things happen. They try to get their beautiful daughter Elly May married. Their nephew Jethro gets a high education, highest in the family– he completes school through the sixth grade. Granny has her fights with Mrs. Drysdale and gets romanced by various men. Jed takes control of a movie studio. They travel to New York, Washington and England. They make silent movies. And they make a few good friends.

The series is about a poor backwoods family transplanted to Beverly Hills, California after striking oil on their land. A Filmways production created by writer Paul Henning, it is the first in a genre of 'fish-out-of-water'-themed television shows, and was followed by other Henning-inspired country-cousin series on CBS. In 1963, Henning introduced *Petticoat Junction*, and in 1965 he reversed the rags to riches model for *Green Acres*. The show paved the way for later culture-conflict programs such as *The Jeffersons, McCloud, The Nanny, The Fresh Prince of Bel-Air,* and *Doc.* Panned by many entertainment critics of its time, it quickly became a huge ratings success for most of its nine-year run on CBS.

Jed Clampett, played by Buddy Ebsen, is one of the most lovable yet complex characters ever created by the television industry. On the surface, Jed Clampett doesn't seem to be the type of character that merits much attention.

After all, he's just a simple, unschooled backwoodsman from the hills who's lived in a shack all of his life, and by pure dumb luck comes into a fortune which doesn't seem to change him one bit. This is what makes Uncle Jed such a wonderful character.

Jed Clampett has pride and honesty: qualities that come through constantly, and nothing will divert Uncle Jed from remaining true to himself or altering the way he treats everyone: with openness, honesty and a real desire to be hospitable. He commands respect, and is respected; not only by his immediate family who are utterly devoted to him, but even by that ridiculous and conniving banker (Mr. Drysdale) who, despite his air of superiority, reveals episode after episode what a buffoon he is compared to the calm and self-assured Mr. Clampett.

In contrast to Uncle Jed's gentle wisdom stood Jethro Bodine, played by Max Baer, Jr., the biggest sixth-grader to ever grace the boob-tube. It's hard to imagine the show without this lovable and boneheaded backwoods bumpkin.

Also, it should be noted Jed Clampett protects and cares for not only his daughter Elly Mae (Donna Douglas), but also his nephew and mother-in-law, Granny Daisy Moses (played by the inimitable Irene Ryan). The latter two were a constant challenge to Jed's patience, which he never lost. Uncle Jed made *The Beverly Hillbillies* a classic.

If brains was lard, that boy
wouldn't have enough to grease a skillet.
Jed Clampett (referring to his nephew Jethro)

OUR GANG

By Thomas F. Matt

One of my fondest memories in the mid-‘60s was watching the *Our Gang* television show on channel 50 while we visited our grandparents in the downriver area of Detroit. For much of my elementary years, we lived in Bay City, Michigan which, in those days, you were lucky to get the three ‘major’ networks at all, let alone any other television programming. Visits to the Detroit area allowed a temporary respite from all of that, because they had so many more TV channels, particularly CKLW channel 50 which was actually broadcast from Windsor, Ontario. I vividly remember running into my grandma’s house to watch all of our favorite shows. It was magical.

A quick side-note to any younger readers: you may find it hard to believe today, with the internet and cable TV, but television programming was strictly a distance thing. If you lived sort of close to the station, you received the station over the air, no wires. It was called an antenna or the semi-famous ‘rabbit ears’ (if you don’t know what that is, ask someone over forty years old).

Our Gang– The first production at the Roach studio in 1922 was a series of silent short subjects. It really is incredible to me how material like the *Our Gang* movie shorts comes from such a long history. It really does prove that great content is simply that: great. Funny content is even better. Hal Roach was a pioneer by putting black and white child actors together, something that was unheard of in those times. Roach would produce the *Our Gang* shorts from 1922 until 1938, when the series was sold to MGM. Hal Roach was a brilliant producer of comedy with many big stars in his stable, including Will Rogers and Laurel & Hardy.

As MGM retained the rights to the *Our Gang* trademark following their purchase of the production rights, the 80 Roach-produced 'talkies' were syndicated for television under the title *The Little Rascals* beginning in 1955.

MGM continued the series until 1944. There were a total of 220 shorts and one feature film. Sound versions of the *Our Gang* series were introduced in 1928, and through the history of the series, over 41 child actors were used.

According to Roach, the idea for *Our Gang* came to him in 1921 when he was auditioning a child actress to appear in one of his films. The girl was, in his opinion, overly made up and overly rehearsed, and Roach patiently waited for the audition to be over. After the girl and her mother left the office, Roach looked out of his window to a lumberyard across the street, where he saw a group of children having an argument. The children had all taken sticks from the lumberyard to play with, but the smallest kid had taken the biggest stick, and the others were trying to force him to give it to the biggest kid. After realizing that he had been watching the kids bicker for 15 minutes, Roach thought a short film series about kids just being themselves might be a success. Come to think of it, many of our outdoor shenanigans as kids were probably the seeds of watching these kids messing around and getting into trouble.

When Roach changed distributors from Pathé to Metro-Goldwyn-Mayer (MGM) in 1927, and converted the series to sound in 1929, the series took off even further. Production continued at the Roach studio until 1938, when the series was sold to MGM, who then continued producing the comedies until 1944. As creation of content would have it, it's been stated that without Roach the series was not as good as the early years, with the child actors acting like adults and not having the childlike spontaneity. Hal Roach had run into a typical financial issue of content providers: competition from feature films. I find it eerily ironic how history continues to repeat itself. What I mean by that is, Roach had a dynamite series of shorts, but as technology moved forward, so did the competition. Much like we had in the fifties with television and film competing for our attention, we now have the internet competing with television. New mediums grow and our hunger for content grows with them.

By the way, how many baby/child commercials are there now that are slapstick in nature? Off the top of my head, I can think of several classics, like the E-Trade commercials that are simply hilarious: kids being kids. The *Our Gang* shorts would continue to influence the world even today.

Roach was a very shrewd man. When he sold *Our Gang* to MGM, he had reserved the opportunity to buy back the rights to the *Our Gang* trademark, provided he did not create any more kids' comedies in the *Our Gang* style or genre. This move would inevitably create a dynasty, as television would launch a whole new generation of avid followers: the Baby Boomers.

THE LITTLE RASCALS

In 1949, MGM permitted Roach to buy back the rights to

the 1927–1938 *Our Gang* shorts, but only if he removed the MGM Lion studio logo and all examples of the names or logos Metro-Goldwyn-Mayer, Loews Incorporated, and *Our Gang* from the reissued film prints. I think about how all of the future will shake out if big studios and/or big business are so narrow-minded that they don't see value. Makes me wonder sometimes. Using a revised version of the series' original name, Roach packaged the 80 *Our Gang* shorts (the shorts with sound) as *The Little Rascals* and had Monogram Pictures distribute the shorts: first to theaters, starting in 1951, and then to television in 1955, under its new name *The Little Rascals* which enjoyed renewed popularity on television. Seeing the potential of the property, MGM began distributing their *Our Gang* shorts to television in 1956. It would be primarily these television versions that we would run to my grandma's TV in downriver Detroit to watch every time we made our pilgrimage from Bay City to her house.

In 1963, Hal Roach Studios, now run by Roach's son Hal Jr., filed for bankruptcy. A stressed neophyte syndication agent named Charles King purchased the television rights to *The Little Rascals* during the bankruptcy proceedings and returned the shorts to television. In 1964, the television rights to *The Little Rascals* were given (I use this term loosely since, as I stated, they were purchased/sold) to Charles King's new distribution division King World Entertainment. It was a company that expressly handled television distribution of the classic Hal Roach *Our Gang* shorts. *The Little Rascals* paved the way for King World to become one of the biggest television syndicators in the world, also distributing *The Oprah Winfrey Show, Jeopardy* and *Wheel of Fortune.* King World has seen success in distributing a variety of television properties and game shows that offer airline tickets, great vacations and other prizes. It can be argued that their success wouldn't have been as great without the storied and successful *Rascals* property. The King empire all started with these wild kids, filmed in the '30s and '40s.

Allow me to digress for just a second. One of the reasons I decided to include the earlier versions of the short films, radio shows and cartoons in our pre-1969 pop history, is again what I feel is giving the due credit to all of the 'back-in-the-day' history. Have you ever wondered why the quality of cartoon animation or the slapstick comedy was so dang good? It was pure– simple as that.

Again, success and shrewdness: who could have figured that filming a bunch of kids being kids would eventually lead to the massive success it did? To list all of the child actors would be a little bit much, with over 41 in total. If you want a comprehensive list, follow this link: *www.picking.com/og-bios.html*

My top five (and I would love to start a comprehensive 'top fives' list from everyone who is a fan) are as follows:

1. Alfalfa (Carl Switzer)

2. Spanky (George McFarland)

3. Buckwheat (William Thomas)

4. Darla (Darla Jean Hood)

5. Pete the Pup (I mean, how could you not like that black-eyed pup?)

Both Roach's *The Little Rascals* package (now owned by CBS Television Distribution) and MGM's *Our Gang* package (now owned by Turner Entertainment) have since remained in syndication, with periodic new productions based on the shorts surfacing over the years, including a 1994 *Little Rascals* feature film released by Universal Pictures.

REFERENCES

en.wikipedia.org/wiki/Our_Gang

www.ramseyltd.com/rascals/history.html

BE PASSIONATE

By Brandon Townsend

Hi, my name is Brandon Townsend. I am a full-time student currently enrolled at Michigan State University, studying Kinesiology and Dietetics. I grew up in the eastern part of the thumb of Michigan, in a little rural farm town called Richmond, and still reside there with my parents and brother during the summers when I am not taking class. Growing up in the small rural town of Richmond really helped me to mature and thrive as a person throughout my years, and one of the things that helped me the most was one simple word: passionate. It is for this reason that I chose 'be passionate' as my contribution to the *Generation Us* book.

The first time I heard the word was during summer vacation, probably around the time I was in my first or second year of middle school. I was vacuuming the house one day, and after I had finished, my mom approached me and we began talking about if I had put any thought into what I may want to do in life when I grow older and become a contributing citizen. At the time, I was quite dumbfounded. I was still in middle school, and the thought had never really crossed my mind. It still seemed so far away from where I was currently. Well, what my mom told me next is something that I, to this day, still have not forgotten. She told me that no matter what I do in my life, even if its vacuuming and cleaning homes, that I need to find something that I am passionate about. Find something that makes you feel like you're never actually at work. Find something that makes you happy, something you actually want to do, something that makes you wake up every day and say, "I want to strive to be the best and do the best that I possibly can." What my mom had told me that day didn't really hit me until a year or two down the road, when I began high school football. Sure, it can be argued that high school football isn't a job, but for me, as a freshman in high school playing my first high school sport (and a sport that I had never played before), it felt like a job. It was a slow start, but as the time and effort that I put in began to pile up, the more it was growing on me and before I knew it I had become quite passionate for the game of football. It felt just like how my mom explained it to me. There wasn't a single morning that I woke up saying, “I don’t feel like playing football today.” I even noticed myself staring at the clock waiting for that final bell to ring so I could go to the locker room and get ready for practice. I loved football, I loved going out on the field and competing hard, getting stronger physically, tougher mentally, all while being around my friends. Football made me a better person. It made me get up every day and say, “I’m going to push just a little farther and reach for better,” because it was easy. My love for football made me want to get better all on my own, which made it fun.

Just like my mother, my father’s take on the word passionate has helped to shape me and make me the person that I am today. The way that my father has used the word passionate to help me is in my work ethic. My father is a very hardworking man. He has held many tough blue-collar jobs throughout his years, and it has rubbed off on me. One of the ways he did this was by using the word passionate. He has explained to me, on more than one occasion, that the reason he has been so successful in his work and gotten to where he is now is because of his passion for his job; and when he means passion, it’s all about the work ethic. When my father explained the word passionate to me, he made it all about how you portray yourself to your employer and how you handle your duties at work. Showing up to work on time (which means being there before the time you are scheduled to start), completing tasks to full completion, and working hard all day long: these qualities show your employer you care about your job and care about making an impact with the work you do. When I got my first job, I took my dad’s advice. I always showed up on time, worked hard and completed my duties thoroughly. It caught my boss's attention and I was rewarded with a dollar raise shortly after being hired into the company. However, I did not stop there. I continued to work hard day in and day out, giving my all to the company, putting in the hours and doing whatever it took to get the job done right and to show my employer I was passionate about the work that I was doing.

The word passionate has helped to shape me into the person that I am today; and for a lot of that, I have to thank my parents. If it weren't for my parents sharing their knowledge with me and opening me up to the idea of being passionate in everything I do, I may not be where I am today.

—

Be Passionate

BE CREATIVE

By Nick Tijerina

It's never too late to bloom, or really, to bloom again; to be creative and create the life you want. Do what makes you happy, but take care of your body and mind first. Meaning simply: read, eat right and exercise. The thought is simple, but the application can be a bit more difficult as we get older and have created a nice comfort zone around us. TV, fast food and comfy furniture can take you on an easy ride to 'slothville' that is hard to get back from, so a little diligence is needed to keep a good quality of life. And really, at our age, that should be our main goal, having a good quality of life. Ok, I'll get off my soap box!

A little about me: I grew up as the eighth child in a family of ten. We were originally migrant workers until my father found a job in a local factory and we planted roots. I grew up in mid-Michigan, went to school, college, US Air Force, several different jobs, two marriages, three kids and a partridge in a pear tree. Oops, I meant now, I am getting ready for retirement and have started to revitalize my dormant art endeavors. I say dormant because my art endeavors have always been with me, but working, growing a family and screwing up a couple of marriages takes some time; so some of the things I've liked to do had to be put on the back burner. Now that my kids are grown, doing well and I've made a halfway decent life for myself, I can do the things I want to do.

With all that, now my plan is to do art as I meander towards the sunset of my life. Drawing, painting, sculpture and writing some bad poetry are the things I like to do. My intentions are to pursue, and hopefully improve, my skills in these areas. I have little desire for fame and fortune, so doing these things are mainly for my own pleasure. I think that is the key. Do what makes you happy. Some people want fame and fortune, others solitude. Find what you like to do and just do it. Do it while you have the time, health and energy. I have been blessed so far in my life that sickness or a bad accident hasn't ruined my body or mind. Those two things are beyond our control, and we don't know when either one of those things will lay the hammer down and ruin the quality of our lives. So, do what you can while you can. You only have so much quality time. My father had a saying that I try to live by all the time:

Do the best with what you got, because that's all you're going to get.

Peace, love and happiness to you.

—

Be Creative

BE HAPPY

By Colin Milner

When we cry out "Happy new year!" we mean it; just about everyone wants to be happy in the new year. As we age, happiness stems less from material possessions and more from health, good relationships and fulfilling activities that keep us engaged in life. In fact, losing their health is the greatest worry of older adults, according to polls conducted by AARP and USAToday/ABC News.

You can take action to have both health and happiness in the new year. Get active. Not just physically active, but intellectually and socially active, too. You'll feel better, improve your health and attitude, and keep your brain working. That'll make you happy!

ACTION PLAN

International Council on Active Aging has taken care of the action items; you need to plan the dates and locations. Get out the paper calendar or iPhone, and schedule 15 minutes each day for the next 4 days to plan how you'll get started. Get your best friend to join in and keep you motivated. Start a Get Active club at your community center or place of worship. Plan on trying these activities over the next few months; don't do everything at once. But work on all of the 10 ways to get active; each will bring you a year's worth of rewards.

1.
INVEST IN A GOOD PAIR OF SHOES AND SOCKS

When your feet are happy, so are you. Foot pain is not a normal part of the aging process, points out the American Podiatric Medical Association. If you have pain in your feet, see a podiatrist (foot doctor), a visit that is likely covered in part by health insurance. Comfortable, well-fitting shoes and socks are a must and worth the investment.

2.
PLAY GAMES

Games keep your brain working and cognitive skills healthy. Plus, it's a fun way to spend time with others. Trivia, math, memory, acting—there is a game for most personalities. You can be competitive or challenge yourself. Traditional board games (chess or Monopoly), crossword puzzles, anagrams, Sudoku puzzles and optical illusions can be played at different skill levels. There are many free games on the Internet, along with sources for those you can purchase. Enter the words 'mind games,' 'puzzles' or 'brain teasers' into your computer's search engine for hundreds of options.

3.
TAKE A WALK OR ROLL

Walk around the block, walk to the store, walk a mile. Walking improves lower body strength, maintains mobility and helps prevent cognitive decline. Research studies have shown that two short walks a day can be as good as a single, longer stroll. Need a personal coach? Get a dog and walk it at least twice a day. Besides getting you out of the house, dogs are loving companions. Once you are walking well, increase your speed and distance.

Need help from a cane or walker or wheelchair? Take your assistive devices on a walk, and ask a friend or companion to join you. While you're out, look around, enjoy the architecture and landscaping and smell the flowers.

4.
STAND ON ONE LEG

Actually, you will work up to standing on one leg by performing balance exercises. Good balance helps you with everyday activities, like reaching into a cupboard, and avoiding falls. When you have confidence in your balance skills, you also have confidence to walk outside, wash the car and visit a museum. Many exercise classes designed for older adults incorporate balance training, and tai chi is gaining a lot of attention for improving balance (as well as reducing fear of falling).

5.
VISIT AN EYE DOCTOR

Failing eyesight is not a given as we age. A study reported in JAMA found that almost all the vision impairment in a large group of people over 60 years old could be improved with corrective lenses. Age-related macular degeneration is the most common vision loss as we get older, but studies have shown that people who smoke cigarettes and are obese are the most likely to get it. (Of course, there are many health benefits once you quit smoking and lose weight). An optometrist can figure you the best plan for your eyes.

6.
INCREASE YOUR PHYSICAL ACTIVITY

Physical activity and exercise do a lot of good things, not only for physical health, but also for maintaining cognitive skills and reducing the risk of dementia. You have to use it or you lose it. Since most people already know this, the question becomes, "how do I get started?"

First, remember that physical activity means housework and yard work (put some effort into it), walking to the store and playing ball with the neighbor kids. Second, make opportunities for activity, like a weekly walking date with a neighbor or friend. Join a wellness center, community center or a health club that has equipment and programs geared to your interests.

7.
SEEK OUT YOUR FRIENDS, FAMILY AND NEIGHBORS

Social connections are good for your emotional well-being. Studies have shown that friendships and the social support network developed at seniors centers, places of worship and neighborhoods not only prevent loneliness, but also provide a ready source of intellectual, physical and volunteer activities. Besides, people with a strong social network lowered their risk of Alzheimer's disease, according to data from the Rush Memory and Aging Project.

8.
EAT A LOT OF FRUITS AND VEGETABLES

Switch to a Mediterranean diet (emphasizing fruits, vegetables, legumes, cereals, some fish and alcohol, and limiting dairy and meat) and you can lower your body weight and cholesterol levels. By the way, the Mediterranean diet has been associated with lowering the risk of Alzheimer's disease. People who eat a balanced plant-based diet don't worry much about counting calories, and gain many vitamins and minerals. You can find fruits and vegetables fresh, frozen, canned, dried and juiced.

9.
LAUGH A LOT

Laughing increases circulation, immune system defenses and mental functioning while decreasing stress hormones. Watch comedies or read a humor book and the comics. Not finding these funny? Then try an exercise recommended by the World Laugher Tour (www.worldlaughtertour.com/). Take a deep breath, then exhale with a big sigh ("Haaaaaa...."). Put your hands at your cheekbones and "hee hee hee hee hee," move your hands over your heart and "ha ha ha ha ha," then place hands on your belly for a "ho ho ho ho ho." Now you're warmed up and ready for spontaneous laughter. Try this with your younger kids or grandkids and let the jokes begin.

10. GET ENOUGH SLEEP

When life gets hectic, adequate sleep seems to fall by the wayside. Don't let it go. Get your seven to eight hours of sleep each night. Insomnia affects almost half of adults 60 years and older, states the National Institute on Aging, making it the most common sleep complaint. If you have trouble falling or staying asleep, make a few changes in your habits, such as skipping daytime naps, adopting a nighttime routine and starting a regular exercise program. Try listening to music, too. By the way, changing your habits is more successful at improving sleep than taking medications.

Did you notice that virtually every activity improves your mental health and reduces the risk of dementia? By increasing your levels of physical activity, social interactions and intellectual engagement, your new year plan of activities that will increase your health and happiness.

Be Happy

THE BULLY IN MY LIFE

By Thomas F. Matt

Cyberbullies do not need direct physical access to their victims to do unimaginable harm.

Anna Maria Chavez

We moved around a lot when I was young, elementary-school-age young. And being the oldest child of five, I never had the benefit (I always was envious of kids that had older brothers and sisters) of an older sibling. My mom and dad were in a dysfunctional relationship from their beginning. Mom was 16 when she married my dad, and I came along a year later; my brother another year later and my sister two years after that. So our beginnings of a family were bound to be trying, if not complete anarchy when a mom has three kids and she is 21, with two more coming in a few more years. Yes, dysfunctional: you could say that.

In my parents' defense, they did the best that they could and we never went for naught. This scenario is why my dad worked so hard at climbing the ladder to lower-middle-class citizenry. Always looking for the bigger paycheck led to moving a lot. I attended five elementary schools in six years, with a stint in the Catholic schools mixed in with some really hard-assed nuns. Wild kids like us, well, we were in for a rough time with their leadership. And the constant changing of schools led to insecurities and becoming a target: a target of bullies.

My experience with being bullied started early, and really was a character-changing time. Coincidentally, this led to becoming lifelong friends with a kid who stuck up for me, and protected me. Over forty years later we still remain close friends. Thank you, David Franco, for befriending me. I was a mouthy little white kid in the sixth grade, which got me into my fair share of trouble. When we moved to Lansing, Michigan in 1970, I was destined for getting picked on, and I did. Life can be rough, but bullying is not to be allowed, ever!

The National Center for Education Statistics reports that there has been a twenty-one-percent increase in bullying since the center began tracking it in 2003, a frankly sobering statistic. With reportedly a child bullied every seven minutes, and 160,000 children in the United States missing school each day for fear of bullying, sadness and deep heartache should be felt in everyone. One in ten children drop out of school altogether because of bullying. Clearly, something needs to be addressed.

Even older people go through this. *Generation Us* is no place for this kind of behavior at any age.

ADULT BULLYING: PHYSICAL BULLYING

This refers to the use of physical intimidation, threat, harassment and/or harm. Examples of physical bullying include physical attack, simulated violence (such as raising a fist as if to strike, or throwing objects near a person), extortion, date rape, marital rape, domestic violence, sexual harassment at work, personal space violation, physical space entrapment, physical size domination and numerical domination (ganging up on a victim).

I had my bully, and it was excruciating. Not only the bully, but the intimidation I felt.
Robert Cormier

TANGIBLE/MATERIAL BULLYING

Using one's formal power (i.e. title or position) or material leverage (i.e. financial, informational or legal) as forms of intimidation, threat, harassment and/or harm. In these scenarios, the bully uses his or her advantage in stature and/or resources to dominate and control the victim.

The greater the power, the more dangerous the abuse.
Edmond Burke

VERBAL BULLYING

Threats, shaming, hostile teasing, insults, constant negative judgment and criticism; or racist, sexist or homophobic language.

The scars from mental cruelty can be as deep and long-lasting as wounds from punches or slaps but are often not as obvious.
Lundy Bancroft

PASSIVE-AGGRESSIVE/COVERT BULLYING

This is a less-frequently-mentioned form of bullying, but in some ways, it's the most insidious. With many bullies, you can see them coming because they are quick to make their intimidating presence known. A passive-aggressive or covert bully, however, behaves appropriately on the surface, but takes you down with subtlety.

Examples of passive-aggressive/covert bullying include negative gossip, joking at someone's expense, condescending eye contact, facial expression or gestures, mimicking to ridicule, deliberately causing embarrassment and insecurity, social exclusion, professional isolation and purposely sabotaging someone's well-being, happiness and success.

CYBERBULLYING

Many types of tangible, verbal and passive-aggressive behavior mentioned above can be conveyed online via social media, texting, video, email, online discussion and other digital formats. Identity theft is also a form of cyberbullying.

The American Psychological Association defines bullying as "a form of aggressive behavior in which someone intentionally and repeatedly causes another person injury or discomfort. Bullying can take the form of physical contact, words, or more subtle actions."

A bully may utilize one or more methods to inflict harm, while deriving wretched pleasure from the suffering of the victim. In the *Generation Us* society there is no room for childhood or adult bullying. Research shows that those who have experienced bullying are twice as likely to go on and bully others. Often, it's used as a defense mechanism and people tend to believe that by bullying others, they will become immune to being bullied themselves. In fact, it just becomes a vicious cycle of negative behaviors.

Those who bully are more likely to feel like their friendships and family relationships aren't very secure. They are more likely to feel like those who are closest to them aren't very supportive or loving or make them do things that they don't feel comfortable doing.

REFERENCES

us.ditchthelabel.org/why-do-people-bully/

psychologytoday.com/blog/communication-success/201701/the-5-most-common-types-adult-bullying

PART 3

LOVING

LOVE QUANDARY

By N.S. Tijerina

PART 01 – LOVE MUSE

I think of you all day.
The smell of you stays with me long after you're gone.
Your smile still glows in my mind.
Your eyes smile and make mine smile too.
You feel so good in my arms, I can't believe
how lucky I am.
I am walking on clouds, with a feeling I've never known
And if I have ever known this feeling,
it was never this good.
The sensory delights, the emotional highs,
The sigh of a comfort that had been lost
or maybe never found before.

PART 02 – TAINTED ME

But this goodness, this wonderful feeling,
Is it really for me?
I'm tainted and she is pure.
If we stay together and get closer,
She will share my taintedness.
If I go, she will remain pure.
We may have already gone too far.
She regrets that we did.
She told me so.
That really hurt.
Yes, it hurt, but I understand why she said it.
She doesn't want the taint either.
She's known for sure, since I knew for sure,

About the taint, but she is still with me,
Probably fighting the same mental battle as I.
But maybe luck has it that the taint wasn't shared
In our small physical union.
Maybe if I get away from her now she will be spared.
I have been more honest with her than anyone before
But she is better than anyone before,
I knew that from the moment I met her
And I wanted things to be so right,
So honest, So pure.
But when you're tainted, stained from your past
Your past comes back to bite you,
And gives you what you deserve
Or maybe takes away what you don't.
I don't want to taint myself any further.
I want a clean and pure soul
A clean conscience, from now on.
To have that though will hurt,
Hurt terribly.
I should send her on her way
To stay pure and untainted.
I cry as I write this because the thought
Of losing the best thing is not pleasant,
Not in the least.
But in good conscience, this is what I should do.
Is my conscience good?
Am I going to make my taint worse?
By knowingly staining her with my taint
She would have to let me,
But does that make it any better?
My brain is a scrambled egg
Between what I want and

What I SHOULD do...
I guess it's up to me make that call,
Film at 11!!

BE ACCEPTING

By Thomas F. Matt

As the generational and intergenerational worlds become more complex, many in the media love to portray a dichotomy between the older populations (G.I. Generation, Boomers, Generation X). With the oldest (G.I. Generation) being born in 1901, and the youngest (Generation X) in 1979, you have an age group from 38-116 years old. You can easily see how values and cultures have shifted. With the oldest Millennial being 37 years old in 2017 and the youngest of Generation Alpha now being born, there is plenty of room to define behaviors and societal habits that can transcend during the 21st century. Much has been said and written about the 'directing' and 'guiding' of Millennials. I would like to think this is a great opportunity to set society up in a positive light. Managing and teaching the Millennials, Gen Zers and Alphas should be a snap, right?

Be Accepting is a start.

So how do we manage/teach Millennials? It's a question

confounding employers and parents across the globe. We need to ask some questions: finding a solution to an issue involves defining it. Here are a few questions to ponder:

- Are Millennials really that hard to manage?
- What do Millennials want from life?
- How do we (older populations) positively impact behavior and morale?
- Can we be more accepting and empathetic?
- Can a truly judgment-free society exist?

Every generation is affected by events of their history. For example, the Depression helped build the mindsets and behaviors of being frugal. Rationing was embedded in our culture, radio carried entertainment and news. In the 1950s we had *Leave it to Beaver* and *Father Knows Best* and the proliferation of television. The 1960s brought us the Hippies, Vietnam and the Civil Rights movement. The 1970s were Nixon, Watergate, lack of trust in government and of course the Arab oil embargo. The 1980s brought us cell phones and women's rights. The 1990s was the beginning of the connected computing age, with the first web browser Mosaic being born in 1993. The turn of the century brought Y2K, social media and ubiquitous connectivity. It was the first time technology really was a dominating force. Cell phones, different parenting styles and their strategies made an impact on our children. We were the first helicopter parents and participation awards became the norm. These are not good or bad; it was just defining how young people would see the world. Events have shaped our world. Now, speed and dissemination of news and constant chatter makes our lives faster and more complicated. Everyone is involved and connected, instantaneous gratification and engagement is the norm!

Understanding how a generation grew up, how we Boomer and Gen X parents over-coddled and 'Purelled' everything for our kids, begs the question of accountability; trouble in school: it must be the school's fault, the teacher's fault, never MY kid's fault!

When Ashley (our eldest daughter) was in the 5th grade, she was in a class of high achieving hellions: you know the types of kids, smart as heck, wild and crazy. Well, the school, Elmhurst Elementary, had this long-standing Halloween tradition of the kids doing this block-long parade in their costumes. The whole school would partake. It was a massive deal. Well, Ashley's class of high-achieving troublemakers were pushing the envelope, and her teacher, Mrs. Lorencen (we loved her) pulled the plug! Oh my gosh, you would have thought the end of the world had occurred– parents were outraged. I was the only parent who wrote a letter (yes, even then I was a letter person), supporting her move. It took major coconuts on her part to do this, but she knew that the coddling of these kids, as great as they all were, would be detrimental to their growth. Sometimes tough love has to occur for any meaningful change. So whose fault is it when our kids leave the nest and get slapped in the face by reality? The shock to their system: things weren't going according to the plan, damnit! We all want the same results, better for my kids than I had right?

Are we at a tipping point? Do we confuse 'taking care of' our kids with offering too much affirmation on their greatness, participation trophies and medals, pats on the heads and the backs? We should ask ourselves, "Are we lowering the bar?" In some respects, we did! We did lack consistency in raising our children, this lead to their confusion and anxiety. No wonder they are skeptical and hate the 'helicoptering' even though we mean well. We spoil the crap out of kids and then turn them loose in the world without the tools necessary to become functional adults, and then what? The trap door opens and they fall through. Shame on us!

Time to regroup, and time to 'be accepting.'

Great cultures are built on talking to each other. Consistent behavior and a genuine desire to work together builds the bridge of trust. Trust between generations begins with good practices, innocuous conversation and helping the 'perceptional' belief systems flourish. Coaching up people is a great example of acceptance.

Not only should we give feedback, we should also be receptive to it. By doing this, we strengthen the bonds between all of us and we encourage knowledge transfer.

Today's younger generations (we are speaking about Millennials, but if the generational shoe fits...) struggle to develop deep meaningful relationships. Technology's prevalence in their lives has created a personal disconnect. Many of our children's relationships are superficial and lack the deep support needed to, again, flourish. Countless numbers of our children turn to the 'feel good' of a social media fix, getting likes, followers, texts (sometimes fighting over responses). Ghosting and FOMO reign supreme.

What are ghosting and FOMO, you ask? Basically, they're

the destruction of the social fabric and skills necessary to have meaningful relationships. Ghosting is a social media trend where you just stop connecting with another person: poof, gone. FOMO is even worse, it is the 'fear of missing out' as they watch their 'friends' doing things and sharing pictures and feel-good moments on social media. Our young people are left wondering, "why I can't be there/ have those," and "what's wrong with me?"

Did you know that the demographic with the steepest increase in suicide is girls ages 10-14, and that this statistic has tripled in the past fifteen years? Girls spend 40% more time on social media and electronic devices than boys do. These devices are addictive and blend into coping mechanisms. Did you know that children need more of the feel-good dopamine neurotransmitter because the constant barrage of technology robs their young brains of balance? The constant connectedness wears them out.

Tech is not the devil; it is just a way of life. How about some positives to talk about here, and let's give Millennials some due credit please! Millennials do speak up at work where the older generations would just take it and suffer in silence. They care deeply about the environment, are hustlers who are never complacent. They handle multitasking with ease (although often get berated for having short attention spans), they are the most educated and are supremely creative. All of us together want to feel that our lives have meaning. So what are some solutions? How can we become more accepting?

First understand that it is never too late to change and become better versions of ourselves; heck, my personal goal is to get a little bit better every day, and it's the incremental changes that can become sustainable. You and I can become better leaders. Become the leader you wish you had and then become better! With this mindset, we all can become better versions of ourselves, learning from the good and the bad. Ask yourself, "What am I doing to encourage change, and to find solutions in being more accepting?"

By coaching people up, by offering membership into our tribe and family, we not only build confidence; we build cooperation, collaboration and community. We build love and trust, but best of all, we find solutions. Yeah, we helicoptered, gave out medals and tried to provide a better life than we had, but we had good intentions. Let's not forget that our young people are the future, we love them and we owe them a break or two. If we do this, we build this thing called *Generation Us,* and that is a great thing!

——

Be Accepting

BE EMPATHETIC

By Colin Jackson

If you admire somebody you should go on 'head tell 'em.
People never get the flowers while they can still smell 'em.
Kanye West, *Big Brother*

Humans have always struggled with empathy. As self-focused beings, we sometimes can't understand others' feelings. To get where someone else comes from takes time and effort. Most of the time, it's much easier to center on our viewpoint instead of placing ourselves in another person's shoes. If we're right, we can comfort ourselves. We don't ask if it matters as much as being compassionate and empathetic. Empathy means being the bigger person. We seldom follow through in a genuine attempt, and that's a problem. Frustration comes naturally when someone falls short. Almost everyone's trying their best already– it's our job to help make each other's best better.

Empathy is hard. It may appear easy, but it's not. The easiest way to describe empathy is "feeling with." Without wearing someone's shoes, it's difficult to tell someone's journey; let alone imagine what that person's feeling. I went to school with a kid that overdosed on heroin. I didn't know him. I don't believe I ever said more than an awkward "hey" to him when I walked past him in the hallway, if our eyes met. As far as I know, he dropped out. After I graduated, news came out that he OD'd. I was video chatting with my friend shortly after and his death came up. She mentioned that his passing put things in perspective. It may have felt like a bad day, but someone nearby had the worst day of his life every day.

That story isn't to say my empathy as a stranger could have saved his life. It's not my place to make that claim or assumption. Instead, it demonstrates a type of thinking for when conflict arises. We gain nothing from judging one another for how we carry ourselves. Judgment minus reflection avoids dealing with problems head-on. To simply conclude 'this is bad' or 'this is good' without looking at the surrounding circumstances would be lazy. Doing so would serve as an excuse not to take the time to understand where someone is coming from or why one feels the way one does. We choose to take the easy road for our own sake in those moments.

Growth requires choosing the harder path. Literature, religion and proverbs point to this. Being understanding can mean fighting a natural reaction. Going down the road less taken sounds scary because it is, though no less important. Actor Michael K. Williams hosts a television show called *Black Market*. In its trailers, he speaks of wanting to show a window "to understanding why people do things they do– where that desperation comes from." For him, that meant spending time with gun smugglers, poker house operators, drug addicts, carjackers and others that society deems criminal.

Views of the humans behind what easily seems like inhumane behavior made the show important. It's not always apparent why someone feels the need to steal a car, and it's certainly easy to label anyone who does a 'bad' human being. A simple label, though, doesn't do anything to curb the desire to steal cars. Sneering doesn't help people move toward a better life than that of a drug-addicted shoplifter. Ignoring someone's potential because of their mistakes and current situation ends up costing everyone. People fall. They find themselves in bad places and do bad things. Recognizing when to help people in those spots and make their best better advances society.

It's important to treat each other as humans first instead of adversaries or objects. Chance the Rapper demonstrates this perfectly in the second half of his two-part tale *Pusha Man/Paranoia* from 2013's *Acid Rap.* In it, he laments on life inside Chicago, a city reporters and outsiders dubbed 'Chiraq' based upon the amount of violent deaths. Commonly, outsiders complain about the violence and deem those that live in the thick of it as savages. Chance offers a different perspective on this central to the idea of empathy: *I know you scared / You should ask us if we scared too / If you was there / Then we'd just knew you cared too,* Chance calls out to anyone listening. His hometown didn't need condemnation and fear, it needed love.

Society doesn't improve when our initial response to disagreement is to fight. When we disagree or perceive something as completely wrong, empathizing and trying to learn why others feel that way brings us closer. There's no way for us to know if the person that seemed rude over the phone or behaved curtly is having a worse day than us or dealing with more than us. We can find out, though, if there's anything we can do to help them find a better mood. Once we can see how they came to those results, maybe our own perspectives can shift. If we still hold the way we feel and their perspective doesn't change, we at least know we tried, and hopefully find ourselves with more respect for each other.

Social media has helped to expose the social lack of empathy. Less practiced, empathy thrives on immersion into opposing views and experiences. Tailored content on our social media feeds fixes it so that we rarely see anything we disagree with. Many liken it to an echo chamber. Challenges are necessary to grow. In a world where we only see what we agree with, we don't have those same challenges. Thus, when confronted, it's a natural reaction to go into attack mode instead of listen mode. People choose to listen to talk back, rather than to listen to understand. None of this leads anywhere. All this lacks compassion.

Occasionally, hashtags poking fun at Millennials trend on Twitter. They point out the usual stereotypes about my generation being lazy, addicted to our phones, unfocused and unable to carry a conversation, etc. Many of these are true and, at the end of the day, they are mostly jokes. Roles almost always reverse when Millennials return the favor by teasing older generations for using a young people's platform to rag on them. Young people respond by adding the fact that older generations built the world that shaped Millennials' habits.

This exchange misses the reasons each side feels the way it does. It also misses the parts each generation can offer. My generation earned the nickname 'The Participation Medal Generation.' Members of previous generations call us soft, and complain about participation awards. They don't try to see why inclusion has value to us. The world can seem like an unforgiving place stacked against success. By solely labeling Millennials as soft or lazy, older generations miss just how hard and competitive our world is and how impossible it really is for a young person to be lazy and successful. Again, ignoring potential. If my generation ignores the wisdom other ones have gained, we lose that knowledge in favor of being hard-headed.

Identity has caused major problems between generations. Gender and sexual identity seems to rank among the worst. A debate over a concept more complicated than society credits doesn't feel right here. Instead, I will take the approach that people can self-identify as whatever gender or sexual identity fits them best. It's not my place, nor anyone else's, to put a value judgment on another person's experience, so I won't. Seeing see how hard things are for people because they're themselves is enough for me to recognize I am not them.

Many find fluid gender and sexual identities hard to understand or swallow. Acceptance can come down to empathy. Life is tough for people that aren't considered 'normal.' For many transgendered individuals, life can be impossible as they often face violence, higher rates of homelessness and a social stigma, among other hardships. Rather than judge a group in these situations, we can put ourselves in their shoes and imagine what life would be like facing those same hardships because of something about ourselves we can't change.

Parents can have a hard time dealing with a child revealing their true self. My friend stayed closeted to his family until recently. His immediate family took it hard. From the outside, it seemed like his parents centered on their own point of view. In his words, "they are trying to get over it and ignore it." Instead, they could have focused on trying to feel what their son was feeling, and trying to understand how hard it must have been for him to be himself. Once he posted a Facebook status announcing his orientation, I scrolled through the comments. In the small sample, I saw family members of his that seemed supportive and willing to learn, though maybe not entirely sure how to react. That's the type of attitude more people need to have.

Choosing empathy means asking, "what are they feeling" instead of, "why don't they see it my way?" It also entails taking the hard path. It requires using every bit of patience. In the end, it means working towards growth rather than to be right. It can come naturally when we see someone upset because they lost out on a job or a promotion. Familiar moments that have frustrated us the most are the times we need to exercise empathy the most. It does us no good to exert our anger on someone else because of a disagreement. It does us much better to understand someone else's position and work together for a better solution.

———

Be Empathetic

BE CONNECTED, BE A CONNECTOR

By Thomas F. Matt

The allies you enlist matter more than the power you exert. Organizations that make the most dramatic progress are the ones that invite ordinary people to make extraordinary contributions, and whose leaders are as humble as they are hungry.
Bill Taylor, *Simply Brilliant*

One of the greatest compliments anyone ever gave to me was calling me a 'connector.' That is one tag that I love, and surely want to perpetuate. Maybe it all started because as a kid we moved around so much. Five elementary schools in six years will do that, especially as an oldest of five children. You develop a certain resiliency as a child to fit in, be liked, or make friends. I found that being good in sports usually translated into a group of built-in friends; teammates tend to have each other's backs.

I needed this as a kid. I believe internet-connectedness has diminished the face-to-face 'golden rule' of socialization, and that we are becoming asynchronous victims of our technology. There are choices, and there is an upside that can enhance intergenerational cooperation.

The radio program would never have become what it is now without reaching out, connecting and building relationships with our family of experts. Heck, this book would never have even been born without being 'connected' to our guests. With the barriers to entry removed, for example, hosting an award-winning radio program from a home studio, being connected through broadband to the internet and the world is great.

I find it really interesting that in the 21st century, work and connectedness are so inextricably commingled. According to Mort Zuckerman's 2014 Wall Street Journal op-ed essay, *The Full-time Scandal of Part-time in America,* there are 28 million part-time workers in the U.S. and, "only 47.7% of adults in the U.S. are working full-time." This certainly is a precursor of sorts that people need to recognize. The scope and scale of work has evolved, and being connected is imperative! John Sculley, former CEO of Pepsi and Apple, writes in his book *Moonshot,*

The millions of part-time workers have been decoupled for whatever reasons from full-time employment with one employer. This is an early indicator that people will need to create their own jobs, because there won't be enough companies or other organizations hiring as many people who need jobs.

Mr. Sculley adds,

Necessity is the mother of invention. People will need to be resourceful, and will lead many to become independent contractors or entrepreneurs.

In the 'Sharing Economy,' connectedness will reign. People will share talent, services, goods and communities of interest will become the norm, in life and business.

THE NEW REALITY

Author Mitch Joel shares these stats and facts (which completely blow my mind) in his book, *CTRL ALT Delete:*

- Google's advertising revenue is bigger than that of the entire U.S. print industry. *(Business Insider)*
- 2/3 of Apple's revenue comes from products it released after 2007. *(Interesting Snippets)*
- Amazon's annual revenue is greater than half of the worlds' GDP. *(PC Magazine)*
- Amazon has enough warehouse space to fill over 700 Madison Square Gardens. *(Business Insider)*
- Amazon owns more North American E-commerce than Office Depot, Staples, and Dell Computers combined. *(PC Magazine)*
- In 1999, 38 million people had broadband Internet access. Today, 1.2 billion have it on their phones. *(Simon Khalaf, Flurry)*

- Facebook has nearly half of its 150 million daily visits from mobile phones. *(Constant Contact)*
- More people have a mobile subscription service than access to safe drinking water and electricity in our world. *(Business Insider)*
- Kickstarter has helped launch over 98,000 new products and has raised $521 million in just four years. *(Kickstarter)*
- Reddit has 62.3 million unique visitors per month, up to 4.4 billion page views per month, and its users spend an average of 39 minutes on the site per visit. Reddit has only 22 employees. *(Business Insider)*

Becoming an 'Adaptive Innovator,' as John Sculley wrote, enables the barriers to entry to tumble down. Clayton Christensen wrote in his book *The Innovator's Dilemma* that disruptive innovation is the change agent and catalyst that will shape all business. *Generation Us* creates a smoother playing field for those who reach out, stay connected and build their personal connectedness. John Sculley wrote,

It's about why this is the best time in history to build these (disruptive and new) businesses– because the convergence of amazing technologies like cloud computing and sensors are enabling radical changes to traditional business processes, which allow for completely disruptive pricing. And it's about the addition of two other incredible technologies, Big Data and mobile devices, like smartphones, which fundamentally shift the power from producers-in-control to customers-in-control.

This may be a surprise to some, but most Baby Boomers own smartphones now, and almost three-quarters of younger Boomers (ages 50-59) own one. Younger Boomers are also more likely to use all capabilities of smartphones; including checking email, getting directions, browsing the Internet, checking the news, even purchasing and playing games on them. I would certainly fall into this group, as does my wife Sandy. With our daily lives revolving around the side game of talk radio, books, speaking and family, we live by our smartphones. At least I do not sleep with it, thank goodness. Yes, being a connector certainly requires me to be connected, and truthfully, I like it.

The network effect of services and 'connectedness' of the world through the Internet of Things radically shifts the landscape, and makes what I like to call the 'Adjacent Possible' thoroughly exciting. Blending of generational collaboration, cooperation and community leads to all kinds of potentials. Hyper-personalization, for example, in pharmacology, science, medicine, nutrition and transportation, is the game-changer. Blend in communication, entertainment and activities, and well, I think you can easily see why we live in super exciting times.

The Consumer Technology Association estimates that the active-aging market of older American adults and their family members could reach 85 million: an estimated 25-billion-dollar market opportunity will grow to an estimated $43 billion by 2020 in the technologies for safety and smart living, health care, fitness and wellness.

"Technology is fundamentally changing the way we live – and active aging tech can dramatically improve our lives as we age," says Gary Shapiro, president and CEO of Consumer Technology Association. "These innovative, connected technologies not only enable seniors to live safer, healthier and longer lives– whether through personal health technology or remote monitoring solutions– they also allow their caregivers to be more closely connected while they care for their aging loved ones. More, these consumer benefits can translate into billions of dollars in savings for the U.S. healthcare industry."

This view was echoed by AARP's report projecting that products and services may be adopted by over 100 million people by the year 2020. The technologies that could create $34 billion in market revenues are for physical fitness, medication management, behavioral health, new care delivery, smart aging, social engagement, diet and nutrition safe living and care guidance.

The number of people in the oldest age group (over 70) is projected to grow from 5.8 million in 2010 to 8.7 million in 2030. In 2050, this group is projected to reach 19 million. Even as they approach the oldest old, the Baby Boomers will continue to have an impact on the age structure of the U.S. population. In 2050, those aged 85 and over are projected to account for 4.3 percent of the U.S. population, up from 2.3 percent in 2030s projection.

The need to educate the tech-savvy student is here to stay, and the need to assist the elders is as well. Technology serves as a bridge between older and younger generations, as one group helps the other break down barriers and connect families and friends. It is the collaboration of the generations that will create a dynamic and influential program.

The blending and removing of lanes of the generations is growing and fast. Until recently, Silicon Valley didn't pay much attention to older people. Entrepreneurs in their twenties and thirties mostly dreamed up solutions for people their own age.

Stephen Johnston, of the innovation network Aging2.0, says that's starting to change. As would-be startup founders seek novel markets, hundreds of 'age-tech' startups have emerged in the last year or two. The group's recent 30-city pitch event, 30in30in30, attracted applications from 300 companies. The problems on the minds of these innovators aren't to do with dating or food delivery/take-out– they're more concerned with problems like how to manage daily drug regimens, cope with dementia and create communities for the over-60 set.

Johnston co-founded Aging2.0 three years ago. It has since organized 170 meet-up events, opened volunteer chapters in 30 countries and signed up 30 companies for its own accelerator program. In return for 2-3% equity stake, the startups can access mentors, advice and a panel of older consumers that can provide feedback on ideas and products. Money has started to fly, too. Honor, the company connecting seniors, caregivers and their families, recently raised $20 million: the biggest funding in the emerging category so far.

THE LONGEVITY ECONOMY

The Longevity Economy is redrawing economic lines, changing the face of the workforce, advancing technology and innovations and busting perceptions of what it means to age. Studies demonstrate that the Longevity Economy is a critical driver of the U.S. economy. Through their work, investment activities, consumption and charitable contributions, Americans over 50 are reshaping the landscape of America and driving economic prosperity. As the economy continues to evolve, meeting the needs of the Longevity population will require dynamic approaches in understanding and delivering the types of goods and services in demand. Reports have explored the implications for some of these potentials:

- Acknowledging the spending patterns of the 50-plus cohort: as the group with the largest spending power, the Longevity cohort will influence market demand
- Identifying and responding to trends in the labor market to maximize the productivity of workers over 50: accommodating the need for longer working lives, as people increasingly work in encore careers, will be the key to maximizing productivity levels in the future
- Staying informed of trends in health care: strategies increasing the quality of life of the Longevity population, accommodating their preference for aging in place
- Innovating and adopting new technologies with potential to improve the lives of people 50 years and older
- Understanding how longevity is good for society, in terms of charitable giving and taxes

As the world transitions to a greater reliance on the contributions of the Longevity Economy, it will become an increasingly valuable asset in terms of economic growth and opportunity.

REFERENCES

www.cta.tech/News/Press-Releases/2016/March/Active-Aging-Tech-Can-Help-85-Million-Americans,-S.aspx

www.aarp.org/content/dam/aarp/home-and-family/personal-technology/2016/05/2016-Health-Innovation-Frontiers-Infographics-AARP.pdf

www.census.gov/prod/2010pubs/p25-1138.pdf

www.debt.com/2017/baby-boomers-really-love-smartphones/

www.wsj.com/articles/mortimer-zuckerman-the-full-time-scandal-of-part-time-america-1405291652

www.amazon.com/Moonshot-Game-Changing-Strategies-Billion-Dollar-Businesses/dp/0795343264

Be Connected,
Be a Connector

BE A COACH

By Lisa M. Cini

You may believe that, to be a coach, you must have an understanding of a sport, or even be great at it. By these standards, if there's anyone that should not be a coach it's me. Although I have an athletic build, my sports were cheerleading and volleyball. I cheered in 8th grade and again my freshman year, and then did not make the Junior Varsity team. I then tried out for volleyball, and being 4'11" I could stand under the net. So, as you can imagine, I was not exactly the most prized player on the team.

Finally, I turned my attention to student council and ended up successful in this endeavor. I realized that if you could honor individuals by understanding their dreams, and then motivate them towards a common goal, anything was possible.

Being a coach is the act of bringing out the best in others and groups. Coaching is the practice of building a bridge between someone's dreams and capabilities, building a bridge between team members' desires and towards a common goal. Coaching strengthens the unique abilities of the individuals and weaves them together to create a team that is much stronger than the individuals alone.

Coaching is about seeing the best in others, and challenging them to bring it! Working together with their talents and gifts, they achieve what they never could've alone. We are all meant to be in community and we all yearn to connect with each other on a deeper level. Coaching facilitates and grows these connections.

I've often heard that if you have the most talented individuals, then you don't need a leader, manager or coach. If this were true, then why does every professional sport have a coach? LeBron James, Michael Jordan, Terry Bradshaw, Cristiano Ronaldo, Wayne Gretzky, Hank Aaron and Joe Montana all had coaches. Their coaches ensured that, as a teammate, they were not only being their best, but supporting their teammates in the best possible way toward a common goal. Coaching is essential to any successful team.

In building my multi-million-dollar business Mosaic Design Studio, I was able to hone my coaching skills. In my business we have designers, architects, engineers, contractors, finance teams and the owners. Getting everyone to work together towards a common goal requires coaching. Through the 20 years in my business, I've realized my talent in aligning everyone toward a singular mission and holding them accountable to the plan. Success is the outcome, and lives are forever changed for the better. However, the real test was when I took my goal setting skills that I used with my children, nieces and nephews and my coaching skills that I utilized in business; and applied it to my kids' high school soccer and club teams. I became the 'Mental Coach' for all the teams. The coaches understood that physical talent was only part of winning a game. Mental strength and the ability to problem-solve and have a mission bigger than yourself would equip you not only for the field, but for the game of life.

The interesting thing about coaching is the more you do it, the more you find others stepping up to help and even following in your footsteps to pay it forward. You also learn more valuable skills regarding your own unique talents and how to use them more effectively for the greater good.

Being a coach is an investment: the more I gave, the more I received. But I realized it is just as important to be coached as it is to coach. I invest a serious amount of time and money into being coached. I am a member in groups such as Entrepreneurs Organization (EO), Strategic Coach, Genius Network, and work with Kim White and Ed Rush. Each of these coaching groups challenge me to be my best and give back. I can look at all of my positive growth points in my life and business, and associate it directly to the time and dollars invested into these groups. If you don't currently have a coach, find one. It doesn't matter the category. It could be fitness, health, finance, business, marketing, social skills or whatever. Just get engaged.

WHAT CAN I DO?

Start by getting to know what your talents are and then where you can apply them (the personality tests below are a great start). I started in student council, then went on to church ministries, board positions, goal setting, mental coaching for sports teams and recently even coached a band named Clubhouse. The point is, you're not going to be perfect, but something is better than nothing. You will get better and learn more, and then apply what you know, and so the cycle continues.

HOW?

STEP 1: Understand each team member's unique ability, and help them to be the best they can be. This is done with challenging, positive reinforcement, discovery and accountability. I also recommend using personality tests such as Kolbe, Strength Finders and Wealth Dynamics to create a consistent language for the team and an unbiased evaluation of their unique abilities.

Why is this important? When we see value in ourselves, we can start to see value in others. Fear of being discovered as not being valuable makes us feel worthless. When we fear we will lose our place, we do things to protect our position and sometimes hurt ourselves or others in the process. If we understand our role and the value of that role on the team, then we can lift others up to be their best. Even if this means riding the bench and challenging the star player to be his best in practice and keep him motivated so that he can be prepared for the competition.

STEP 2: Get everyone to buy off on the team mission

over their individual mission.

Why is this important? The team vision must be number one in the hearts and minds of the team. Don't get me wrong, it needs to be aligned with the individual team members' goals and values, but the team must come first or there will be no team. You've seen it happen before where talent loses to heart. Being aligned towards a common goal transcends math. This is where 1 + 1 does not equal 2, it equals 3! Heart is the extra player on the field that gives strength, courage and selflessness to the team as they need it. Heart is what we all love to watch and cheer for. Heart is the 1980 U.S. Olympic Men's Hockey Team.

STEP 3: The key is to get all the players on the team to understand the impact that their individual goals have on the outcome of the whole mission.

Why is this important? The team members may understand their unique ability and the team's mission, but may not be clear on how they all tie together. This is the most critical insight a coach can bring to a team.

Think about a Rubik's cube puzzle– if you try to solve the puzzle by getting your side completed, you will undo some of the work of the other sides. You can only solve the puzzle by understanding how all the sides interconnect and affect each other. The job of the coach is to see and communicate this to the team. If the players trust the coach, then they will be patient, even if they have to wait till their side is solved, because they understand and have bought into the bigger vision.

THE 20 YEAR RULE

Dan Sullivan, one of my coaches, always tells me to associate with people 20 years younger and 20 years older than myself. I have taken this to heart with coaching, both in being coached and coaching others.

The benefit of this 20 Year Rule is the connections made on a deeper level, and in this age of over-communication with little deep connection, we need deep relationships outside of our comfort zone more than ever.

The wisdom and perspective I gain from both groups helps not only to take me out of my Facebook/Starbucks/News Media silo'd view of the world that is framed in such a way to cut out critical information so that we see a distorted view of reality, much like a Picasso painting of a beautiful woman; but also brings me back to reality helping me to see all sides and learn from/relate to them.

When I am coaching 20 years younger, I seem to have more energy, I risk a bit more, I get excited about the possibilities of their future; and in doing so, I gain my creativity back. It's like I get to see flowers bloom for the first time and I am reignited to plant my bulbs for the next season.

When I am coached by 20 years older, I am challenged to value time and relationships over money and goals. I've learned to focus on the journey vs. the end result and to enjoy the creation process along the way. I see all that they are doing, and am encouraged that my life is not winding down, but just being reinvented to what I desire it to be.

Having experienced sides of coaching, I can't imagine life without it. It seems to me that as Napoleon Hill stated in his book *Outwitting the Devil*, the desire of the devil is to get us to drift without any commitment to one direction or another. In this way, we go against ourselves, our God-given talents and our unique abilities, and become unknowingly selfish, without purpose and unable to give. This is a prison of the mind, when we let distraction become the norm. Break free and be purposeful. You were put here for a purpose. You have much to give. All you have to do now is choose to. You were meant for this.

Be a Coach

BE YOURSELF

By Sky Bergman

Be yourself; everyone else is already taken.
Attributed to Oscar Wilde

When we are young, all we want to do is fit in. We want so much to be liked by other people that we sometimes forget who we really are. We try to please and reflect what we see in others. In doing so, we tend to cover up and smother the spark of individuality that makes us who we are.

To be yourself, you must first know yourself. If you feel uncertain about who you really are, look to your passions. Find your passions, your joys, your strengths; and use them to become, more fully, who you are! Listen to your inner voice– it will guide you on your path. Opportunities present themselves, and if you are open to being all that you can be, you will go for it.

At first, following your passion may not be the easiest path, but I promise in the end it will be the most rewarding. It takes great courage on your journey to be yourself and live with your dream. Along the road to discovering yourself, you learn to embrace the temporary setbacks as opportunities and move on.

My grandmother, who lived to 103, was my inspiration and role model. She instilled in me the notion that I could do anything if I believed in myself. At any age, you can reinvent yourself and be true to yourself. As my grandmother used to say, "Age is just a number." As I was approaching 50, I realized that my passion in life had changed; I moved from being a photographer to being a filmmaker quite by accident. Because of my grandmother and my desire to save much-loved memories of her, I started on the journey of producing my first feature-length film, *Lives Well Lived.* In addition to filming my grandmother in the kitchen, (she was an amazing Italian cook!) when she was about to turn 100, I filmed her at the gym because I thought no one would believe that my grandmother is still working out at this age. I asked her if she could give me a few words of wisdom, and that was the beginning of the *Lives Well Lived* adventure, a new chapter in my life.

In our society, the elderly are often overlooked. Yet, who knows oneself better than a person who has lived a long and productive life? After interviewing my grandmother, I wanted to bring that generation to the forefront. Our greatest role models are those living full and meaningful lives in their later years. I had no firm idea of what I was going to do or how I was going to produce my film, but I persevered, and I asked for help along the way. Most successful people have often stumbled along their journey to success, and learning to look at each setback as a lesson rather than a failure was the key for me. It is my positive attitude and my belief in my work that keeps me moving forward on my journey.

Important lessons I have learned along the way: Look at each setback as a valuable lesson rather than a failure. Be vulnerable and open to follow your dreams and your passions. Life is not a dress rehearsal, there is no do-over. Just go for it!

Leave yourself open to new things. Instead of saying why, ask yourself, why not? Follow your passion... It will lead you to your true self.

———

Be Yourself

PART 4

LEARNING

IT'S TEN AFTER LATE

By N.S. Tijerina

It's time to move
It's time to go
Got to get there
But I go so slow

People will be waiting
They are counting on me
And I'm moving so fast

As fast as a tree

They will click their fingers
They will tap their toes
They know who I am
They know the no shows

I got to get moving
Get out of the gate
Hustle that bustle
It's ten after late.

THE MINDSET OF EXCEPTIONALISM-NESS

By Thomas F. Matt

Love yourself first and everything else falls into line. You really have to love yourself to get anything done in this world.
Lucille Ball

I had the pleasure to give my *Ignite Your Life* keynote speech to a group of engineers, business owners, entrepreneurs, educators and governmental leaders. To say I felt like the dumbest guy in the room would be an understatement. As I shared with the group, hanging out in the company of really smart, successful people is a precursor to self-improvement. It was a great day!

Hosted by the Capital Area Manufacturers Council (CAMC) at the Kellogg Center on the campus of Michigan

State University, this social/business gathering brought together men and women who want to see our economy thrive and improve.

For example, I met Jeff Metts, President of Dowding Industries, and his right hand, Executive Director Rebecca Roberts. I met Andy Storm, President and CEO of Eckhart and his Director of Human Resources Stephanie Schanher; Jim Bunn, business services Liaison for Capital Area Michigan Works; and Julius Diaz, Director of Human Resources for Emergent BioSolutions; just to name a few. These executives want to move the needle higher and create positive economic momentum.

The demands of the 21st century workforce are dynamic and intriguing, never before imagined. Working to not only encourage upward mobility, these demands include:

- Engagement
- Learning and education
- Growth (including spiritual, physical and intellectual)
- Goals and the ever-changing need for re-evaluation, creation and modification of them. Using acronyms such as SMART (specific, measurable, attainable, realistic, timely) to challenge us daily on the journey of incremental self- improvement.
- Continual performance evaluation, both on a personal level as well as professional
- Customer-focused employees

Together, building a new mindset of 'exceptionalism-ness'

will overcome many of the obstacles becoming pervasive in the 21st century. This mindset will take collaboration and teamwork, and a new paradigm must emerge to really embrace this potential forward-moving momentum. Multigenerational giving and mentoring, training and sharing must occur for continued upward mobility.

In an article for Time Magazine, Paul Taylor wrote about Millennials and their 'Economic Indignities' where, "unlike their parents and grandparents, this is a downwardly mobile generation (ouch), with smaller incomes, less wealth (ugh), more debt, higher unemployment and fewer homes than their parents' generation had at a similar age." Stepping to the aid of our children, and for some our grandchildren, has never been a more serious issue. The knowledge economy may hold potential, but only in randomized pockets of success– for the vast majority of Millennials, the future could be bleak.

That is, if we don't do something about it!

As I say on my radio talk show Boomers Rock, through adversity grows opportunity. The intergenerational upward mobility and the confidence growth that is necessary for becoming part of the new normal of 'Exceptionalism-ness' is upon us.

The marginalization of certain age groups is the future draining of our talent pool. What will we do to combat this trend?

Generation Us is a start!

The best way to battle betrayal is through giving back, to caring and to loving and reaching out in newer and better ways. The new-new normal is a time of reflection and re-evaluation of our principles. Speaking to the CAMC really opened my eyes to the concern of these business owners and leaders in finding the next generation of talented skilled trades, fabricators and creative builders. Filling the collective pool of talented, 21st-century creative hands-on workers and doers will take ingenuity and effort.

We all may live in the most technologically-advanced world ever, and the Millennials may be the best-educated and omnipresent consumers of technology, but without hands-on functional workers, here in our state and other states in our country (manufacturing employs more people than any other category in Michigan) our way of life will not reach the potential that it can be.

'Exceptionalism-ness' will take all of us to get our house in order and dream better dreams. For example, the *Believe in Amazing– Superintendent Speaker Series* that a group of friends and I are developing will raise the bar to a new level. This group includes Dr. David Hornak, Superintendent of Holt Public Schools, and Brian Town, CEO of Michigan Creative.

In this seminar series, we will share ideas, talk about positivity and acknowledge good things that are occurring in secondary education all while building community outreach and brainstorming the next new-new things. Introducing leaders of industry to students and bringing artistic outreach and inclusiveness to the forefront are just a couple of ideas for our speaker series.

Showcasing all that is good, and working toward and helping everyone achieve greatness, multigenerational in nature, community collaboration in scope, we are going to make a difference.

You just gotta light the kindling to start the bonfire that can be greatness.

Hope begins with faith, and leadership is enhanced with outreach. It will be all of us together that can make an impact. The time is here and the time is right to become 'exceptional!'

Meeting the executives at the CAMC meeting and delivering my *Ignite Your Life* seminar was really a blessing, I thank everyone who attended for their kindness and positive response– it was wonderful.

Let us think about all of these issues, because we can make a difference, we can all be part of the solution. All it takes is faith!

If you would like to continue this conversation, or if you are looking for the spark to light a fire in your organization and people, contact me for availability in speaking to your group or organization.

Let's change the world together.

BE INDEPENDENT

By Thomas F. Matt

SIMPLICITY is the ultimate PERFECTION.

Steve Jobs

As the parents of two girls, Sandy and I worked diligently to instill an attitude that would enable the kids to, as Mr. Spock would say, "Live Long and Prosper." The journey was sometimes filled with significantly deep potholes and detours (ask me about when Ashley snuck a tight 'Bootylicious' T-shirt on under her hoodie at 14 years old– that was drama!) but we did our best. Even if you were not given the gift of parenthood, you can still embrace the mindset of encouraging and teaching young people. It truly is a gift.

I must have told the girls a thousand times, "never be dependent on some dude," and (they will be horrified when they read this) "protect the candy store." I will discuss the first point; let your mind fill in the blanks on the second. I share the same message with all of my college-aged female friends; it is my duty as a dad!

On our laundry room door there is a sign that reads, 'Mom's– Washed, Dried, Folded– Laundry: Same Day Service, Do It Yourself.' Everything in life begins in the laundry room! If we do our kids' laundry for them past, say, the age of 12-14, then we need to regroup and re-evaluate the mission of parenthood. Our job as parents is to build independent human beings!

If a young woman/man/boy/girl is never taught this most basic chore, then how in the hell are they ever going to learn how to mow the lawn, check the oil/air in their car and tires, do dishes, cook food and balance a checkbook? As I have learned anytime we want to solve a problem, we have to identify the problem. No one is perfect, things happen, constraints occur. It comes down to how we deal with it.

Becoming independent is all about resources and working through constraints, roadblocks and problems. By embracing issues, we leverage future stressors, we improve and we get better. We turn roadblocks into open doors, we unlock potential and we enable independence.

There are several types of constraints that can be perceived as roadblocks. Here are a few:

- Money: In business and in life, money is a huge potential roadblock to success. The roadblock works in both directions, having too much money creates laziness and impairs hard work; not having enough can virtually paralyze people into perpetual limiting beliefs. Resilience is born from hard work, grit comes from sticking with it.

- Knowledge: A lack of experience about a particular aspect in life or business can be a restriction, but it also can be an advantage. Again, I want to emphasize my own journey into the land of insecurity in college: the best thing that ever occurred in my life was sucking it up and getting back into it. If I can do it, anyone can!

- Time: The roadblock or constraint of time is another two-lane street. I hear it all the time in the fitness area, "I just don't have enough time," when frankly, you can add time by doing just a few small steps. It is only through incremental change that anything is truly a behavior modifier. Habits are formed in the most imperceptible steps, and the payback can be massive. Investing in yourself empowers you to invest in others. Time is our most precious resource, leverage it in a positive direction and watch what happens.

Here is a challenge to anyone who wants to become more independent: I call this the 'Seven Top Words List.' Write down the seven most important words in your life and analyze this list. Now, what I suggest, is making this a fun exercise– something that stimulates the brain a little. These seven words can have a big meaning to you. Make it broad. If it is a life word, it should hold depth. Order does not matter. Here is my list:

1. Family. My family is everything to me. It is the driver of all that I do and live for. Having a close, tight relationship, and doing all that I can to polish the jewel that is my family, is imperative. Even though I said the order of this list

does not matter, this will always be my numero uno!

2. Health. The importance of health is as wide as it is deep. Doing everything I can to stay on top of my game is critical. Health is totally multifaceted; to keep it simple, I use an acronym in my speaking engagements: ESPM– Eat, sleep, poop, move.

3. Outreach. All of the work we do and the relationships we earn between friends and colleagues leads to the sharing of knowledge. Our whole platform is built around touching souls through media. You never know when or how a message may be a person's catalyst to change. I have seen this many times, and it is amazing!

4. Education. Everything, and I mean everything, that I have accomplished I owe to my education at Michigan State University. It was an incredible opportunity that I was so fortunate to have. Continuing education, lifelong learning, reading and interviews for radio make my life richer.

5. Friends. I have been so fortunate to have a huge number of acquaintances, which then become my friends. This takes time, it is an investment and it is so worthwhile. I love all of my friends.

6. Freedom. Funny word to put in my top seven, however, having the freedom to create, to influence, to grow and to perpetuate our values is wonderful. Working toward financial freedom to do more is the end game, and it is coming! You've just gotta keep working!

7. Optimism. If there is one thing that I would like to be remembered for, it is being optimistic. I have lived in

the darkness of despair: drug and alcohol abuse, broken marriage, single parenthood. When you live through the abusive, self-destructive behavior, survive a life-threatening illness, and then find yourself healthy and happy after overcoming it all, you appreciate life. I am so optimistic every day because I have the six previous words working together.

I hope this list helps you to craft your own list, because to 'be independent' is so worthy of the effort it entails. Never give up on yourself.

Be Independent

THE MIDDLELIVING ECONOMY

By Thomas F. Matt

There are four principal types of economic systems on the planet: traditional, command, market and mixed. Each economy has its strengths and weaknesses, its sub-economies and tendencies, and, of course, troubled histories. In the 21st century, you may as well burn the textbooks because creative destruction is the rule, not the exception!

Traditional economies still create products and services that are an undeviating result of their beliefs, customs, traditions, religions, etc: useful and old-school.

Command economies are an economy in which production, investment, prices and incomes are determined centrally by a government. Dictators and monarchies: for sure dead ducks.

Market economies are those in which decisions concerning investment, production and distribution are based on supply and demand, and prices of goods and services are determined in a free price system. Hanging in there, but losing steam fast.

Mixed economies are economic systems that combine private and public enterprise. Hello! We may have a winner, sort of!

Move over old-school economic philosophies, there are some new Sheriffs in town (notice the plural of 'Sheriff?')

Aaron Hurst wrote about the Purpose Economy, and how your desire for personal growth and sense of community can impact and change the world.

You have the Sharing Economy, (What, never heard of this? Come on, Fred Flintstone!) Companies like Airbnb, Turo (formerly RelayRides), TaskRabbit, Lyft, and of course, Uber; are all examples that even Wilma and Barney would use in Bedrock. Peer-to-peer on growth hormones, basically.

We have the Maker Economy, a technology-based DIY mindset and culture. Crafts, metalworking, with a little bit of tech, or a lot. Chris Anderson of Wired shared his thoughts in *How the 'Maker' Movement Plans to Transform the U.S. Economy* for Time magazine and authored *Makers: The New Industrial Revolution.* Stand tall, makers– this is not just crafting anymore. Etsy is just what the crafter ordered!

The Gig Economy is a mixture of everything. Make some time, find a passion– freelancers everywhere rejoice! Adam Smith called it the Genuine Market in *An Inquiry Into the Nature and Causes of the Wealth of Nations*, during the 18th century!

I have a new one, and this one is going to dominate by using all of the above. A hybrid future rockstar I like to call the MiddleLiving Economy: where encore careers meet your transitional wanderlust. Entrepreneurship is being driven by adults over the age of fifty (my definition of MiddleLiving is 40-85 years old), so the utilization of the Gig Economy leads to profound economic development. Are you ready for this?

Small-scale entrepreneurship is a massive economic driver, and could become the catalyst for changing the way we view retirement. I have always referred to retirement in the 21st century as walking through the front door of the 'ReFirement-Zone.' Here are some facts and figures:

- Some estimate that the rise in entrepreneurship for those 55 and over could increase yet another 20% in the next 10-15 years.
- In every single year from 1996 to 2007, Americans between the ages of 55 and 64 had a higher rate of entrepreneurial activity than those aged 20-34.
- For the entire period, the 55-64 group averaged a rate of entrepreneurial activity roughly one-third larger than their youngest counterparts.
- These trends seem likely to persist: in the Kauffman Firm Survey, a longitudinal study of nearly 5,000 com-

panies that began in 2004, two-thirds of firm founders are between the ages of 35 and 54.

Additionally, Kauffman research has revealed that the average age of the founders of technology companies in the United States is a surprisingly high 39, with twice as many being over age 50 than under age 25 who know how to operate a business (*Education and Tech Entrepreneurship*, Kauffman Foundation Research Report).

And as far as wealth is concerned,

- The 55+ age group controls more than three-fourths of America's wealth *(ICSC)*.
- 78 million Americans who were 50 or older as of 2001 controlled 67% of the country's wealth, or $28 trillion *(U.S. Census and Federal Reserve)*.
- Boomers and seniors have seen a decrease in their median family net worth, however, they still have a net worth 3 times that of younger generations *(Economic Policy Institute)*.
- Baby Boomers outspend other generations by an estimated $400 billion each year on consumer goods and services *(US Government Consumer Expenditure Survey)*.
- In 2009, spending by the 116 million U.S. consumers age 50 and older was $2.9 trillion, up 45% in the past 10 years *(Bureau of Labor Statistics)*.
- Baby Boomers account for nearly $230 billion, or 55%, of consumer packaged goods sales *(Nielsen)*.

- Americans over 55 spend 50% of all vacation dollars in the United States.

- Women over 50 spend $21 billion on clothes annually.

- Baby Boomers take great pride in the appearance of their homes, as 27% have had landscaping done in the past year and are 21% more likely than all American adults to have spent $10,000 or more on home improvements in the past year *(Scarborough).*

- The NAHB predicts the aging-in-place remodeling market to be $20-$50 billion. That's about 10% of the $214 billion home improvement industry.

- 96% of Baby Boomers participate in word-of-mouth or viral marketing by passing product or service information onto friends *(ThirdAge and JWT Boom).*

So, when it is all done, and done correctly, the multigenerational collaboration that is going to occur will benefit everyone, and then some. Economies of scale and scope never dreamed of by Adam Smith or Fred Flinstone, no time for 'Schleprocks.'

Just remember these key phrases: Sharing Economy, Electronic Markets, social media, durable goods, Collaborative Economy, on-demand, collaborative consumption, crowdsourcing, crowdfunding, p2p, internet, e-commerce, Airbnb, Uber, Lyft, Lending Club, Blablacar, WeWork, Instacart, Ola...

You see my point! Time to get on the bus, gang. Time is our most precious resource.

BE PREPARED

AN INTERVIEW WITH MIT'S AGELAB DIRECTOR DR. JOSEPH COUGHLIN

By Colin Milner

At the Massachusetts Institute of Technology AgeLab, the prospect of 'Life Tomorrow' engages a multidisciplinary research team. "The MIT AgeLab focuses not on aging," as might be expected, "but on the future of living," according to a video overview.[1]

Director Joseph F. Coughlin, PhD, founded the research program "to invent new ideas and creatively translate technologies into practical solutions that improve people's health and enable them to 'do things' throughout the life span." Of equal importance is the belief that "innovations in how products are designed, services are delivered, or policies are implemented are [critical] to our quality of life tomorrow."[2]

Dr. Coughlin's area of research includes how demographic change, technology, social trends and consumer behavior drive innovations in business and government. Professor Coughlin teaches in MIT's Department of Urban Studies and Planning and Sloan School of Management's Advanced Management Program.[3] He has been named by the Wall Street Journal as one of the "12 pioneers inventing the future of retirement" and by Fast Company as one of the "100 Most Creative People in Business."

As ICAA's CEO, when I heard that Dr. Coughlin was coming out with a new book in 2017, I wanted to interview him for the Journal on Active Aging to see what fresh perspectives he had for our readers. What thought-provoking comments did this visionary have to share? Here's a taste: Longer life is humanity's greatest accomplishment. Old age is made up. Population aging is a catastrophic event–or not. And, women are the future of innovation.

Curious? Let's dive right in.

———

CM Joe, it's always a pleasure to chat as you have a unique way of expanding my mind. For those who have yet to hear your perspectives on the many issues of aging, a good place for us to start is at the beginning. How did MIT AgeLab come to be?

JC I would argue that the greatest achievement of humankind has been longer life. Looking back 100 years, people in most of the industrialized world and many developing economies are now enjoying 10, 20, 30-plus years of longer life than their grandparents and great-grandparents. And so MIT's AgeLab was started, shall we say, to cash in on the longevity dividend. We seek to develop new ideas, technologies and, indeed, business models that not only create things, but also create experiences to improve the quality of life of older adults and those who work with them.

We started in transportation, around the issue of older drivers– sometimes an issue caught between humor and horror. But, in studying transportation, we realized there was an absence of infrastructure for an older population, or an aging world. As a society, we hadn't thought through housing or transport, work or play. All those big and little things that become life when you string them together. AgeLab became, to my memory, the first multidisciplinary, multi-domain center to seek a new future for old age.

There are many researchers out there doing great things in housing, or care, or transportation. However, to form and to integrate all these things together: that is innovation, and that is the new platform for old age. That's the work we do at AgeLab.

CM Thanks for that snapshot of AgeLab. Let's chat about you for a moment. Your new book, *The Longevity Economy*, is coming out later this year. Why did you write this book?

JC I wrote the book largely because, after starting the AgeLab and working with industries around the world (more than 45 different companies), one of the things I found was that the biggest barrier to inventing the new future of old age was not the availability of technology or the acknowledgement of this big market with lots of money; it was the fact that we were telling the wrong story. I wanted to help change that story.

The Longevity Economy is not just about the size of the market, but the idea that 'old age,' as we conceive it, is the greatest barrier to creating a better, longer life. Frankly put, our concept of old age is made up. It is basically a social construct that originated around 100-150 years ago. During this time, it has wormed its way into how everyone– including business, government, and even the academy– thinks about aging. Business, in particular, plays an important role in defining what's normal at different times of life, from youth and adolescence through middle age.

But at age 65 or so, something changes. The made-up notion of old age, as presented through products and marketing, tells us that it's a time to retire, to withdraw, to stop. But it's not. What I suggest in the book is that it's actually an entire life stage that has yet to be invented, so writing the book is a call to arms for business and for others to look at old age differently. It is, I hope, a wake-up call. An observation that all the pieces are here, the demand is now, and the opportunity started yesterday.

CM Why do you think business and society, in general, have neglected the older consumer and the older population at large?

JC We have to be somewhat kind to businesses and governments and many of our institutions. Think about the following: If life expectancy in 1900 was 47 and today it's well into our 70s, to the point where we know the fastest-growing part of the population is 85-plus, we've never really been confronted by this many older adults with this much education and expectation for their future. And with technology at our disposal to not just live longer, but to live better (and be far more than medicalized better); to have new experiences and new activities to do and new engagement. So I think we've ignored old age because, frankly, it's brand new. Also, business in particular has always had a bias towards youth.

You could say that the Boomers and their parents are reaping what they sowed decades ago– that is, if we market to the 18-30 year old, we've got 'em for life. So why do businesses even need to worry about the older consumer? Well, we found that Boomers were willing to forget car brands at the drop of a hat when those brands did not answer their demands. So, no, you can't assume that if you capture the youth market, you have them for life. Now is the time to understand how to capture the customer across the life span.

Our challenge? We are trapped in our made-up vision of old age. We are trapped into believing that older adults do not have money, that they don't like new things, that they are not educated, and that they're afraid of technology. That paradigm gets in the way of inventing the new old age.

CM How long will we have to wait before people get the message?

JC When the AgeLab started around 2000, Japan and Italy were the only places where I could find an audience as well as resources for an aging-society discussion. Now, at least there are companies out there saying, "Yes, we acknowledge there's an aging population, and they have both the resources and the aspirations to do more." So I am seeing a little change.

That said, those companies that seem focused on older adults are still trying to develop new products with the old vision. That's why we have profoundly medicalized aging. Rather than creating toys for play, we create toys for company. For older adults, we remind you to take your medications rather than creating exercise and services for you to engage with and be productive and make new friends. We focus primarily on the diseases that we can help manage. It's not that those things are incorrect. They are woefully incomplete, however. Business needs to expand its understanding of the older consumer: She is far more than a medical problem to solve.

CM Is it possible that the 'Me Generation' may actually become the 'Forgotten Generation?'

JC Since the Boomers are at the helm of our institutions, businesses and governments, their legacy may be to make those additional 30 years into something to look forward to. To invent a new social contract that says, "If you work very hard for 50 or 60 years, we're not going to send you out to pasture for the next 20 or 30; we're going to prize you as a resource, as an opportunity, as part of society." Boomers, if they act now, have the possibility of giving perhaps their greatest gift to future generations: a new vision of longevity. A vision that views old age not as a time to retire and to ignore and pull away from society, but as another life stage to be invented. Not only can they give the benefit of this legacy to Gen Xers and Millennials and Gen Zers, but the Boomers and their parents will also benefit at the same time.

CM You said something very interesting there: Act now as opposed to later. What happens if we don't act now?

JC Over the last few decades, we've seen an entire industry built around the how-bad-it-is-that-we-have-an-aging-population belief. If you think about some of the books and articles written, such as *Demographic Winter* or *A Perfect Storm*, you'll realize they invoke imagery of cataclysmic events, instead of celebrating our achievement of longer life. Greater longevity is something humankind has wanted since we crawled out of the ooze, yet we've translated it into something terrible. However, if we do not act now, with one Boomer turning 71 every 7-8 seconds in the United States alone, those ominous forecasts will likely come true. We will have bankrupt health plans, insufficient retirement pension plans, inadequate housing and care and the like. But, we have an opportunity– in the US, Europe, Asia, South America and throughout the world– to invent not just a new vision of old age. We have an opportunity to invent a new way to engage the older population to help themselves, to create new products that grow the economy, and to find new ways to engage these individuals to increase the productivity of the workforce, and to delay those periods of life when they can't be productive.

If we act today, we will not only live longer, we will also live better. And, our legacy for future generations will be that we seized the opportunity and saw old age and longer life as a resource, not as a problem.

CM You seem optimistic about the future of aging and the role of business. Why?

JC There are two reasons why I'm optimistic. First, I think we have both a desire [to seize the opportunity] and all the tools at our disposal. The second reason is being anything but optimistic relegates us to a past that is not going to promise a good future. So I believe that business and related organizations, with the catalyst of lead adapters in the consumer market, will create entirely new visions of what to do with those extra years of life.

I am convinced that three things will converge to create an entirely new life stage of products, services, public policies, and experiences that will benefit everyone, not just the very old. They will also improve the social contract for the very young, so we think across the life span as to what our quality of life is, not how long our life is. These three things are:

1. The technologies available to us
2. The expectations of the next generation of older people, especially older female consumers, who are lead adapters today and will continue to be tomorrow
3. The awakening of business to the market and the fact that the longevity economy equates to 70% of the nation's and the industrialized world's disposable economy

CM Old age is going to be something quite different in the near future then?

JC Well, as I said before, old age is quite new in that

we've never had this many people living this long. But there's something else going on as well. What I argue in the book is that we're having smaller families, for instance, so we are going to have to change and reinvent the whole notion of how one stays connected or receives care. We live in more dispersed locations, as 70% of the 50-plus population in the United States lives in rural and suburban areas; this is also happening around the world.

The thing we also have to take into account is that the context of aging has changed as well. We now not only look to technology to improve our lives, we expect it to improve our lives, because we have seen it all through our lives: from something as simple as every new model car, to the power of computing going from the space program into the palms of our hands, to the wearables on our wrists.

So, the technology is there. The numbers are there. The context of how we live and how we relate to our families is there. We also have more education than any generation of older adults in history. This all leads up to what I call the expectations gap: a gaping void between the way Boomers expect to be catered to by business, and how business has historically treated older adults. This next generation of older adults will not be as patient nor as polite as their parents when their needs go unmet; they're going to expect a policy, a pill, a product or something else to improve their lives as they advance in age.

CM If you were to give advice to a young person who is looking at the older consumer from a business perspective, to what would you recommend this individual pay close attention? Should this person even view older ages as population segments or as just a continuation of life?

JC My advice would be: look at old age as a continuation of life, but also really question all your built-in assumptions. Old age is not just an opportunity for a startup to create a new wheelchair, walker, pill-reminder system or sensor to warn if someone has fallen and can't get up. Those things are necessary, and we need to continue to develop them. But if you have verve and intelligence and understand technology, start asking yourself, What new thing can people do with that extra time? What do they want to do? As an example, how do we enable lifelong learning across the life span?

Start re-thinking the fact that life-stage models and market segmentations done by industry are just plain wrong. People are getting remarried and downsizing after age 50. They are running businesses– on average, small business owners are in their late 50s. People are going back to school in their 50s, 60s and 70s. What life stage is that? What segment is that? So throw out your assumptions, and don't be afraid to watch and talk and listen and learn. More importantly, do not run your business opportunities by focus groups. Start thinking about what people are doing, and what else they could do that you could enable with a new technology or a new service, or by working with government in a new public-private partnership.

Lastly, for your own old age, plan for the long haul, take care of your health, and be a lifelong learner– and not just because it's good to keep engaged. Someone coming out of school today is likely to have 4 or 5 different careers, not just different jobs. If you're coming out of school today and looking at the older-adult market– whether it's senior housing, transportation, work, education or any of these things– it is one of the most exciting times to be graduating. Because you're not just working for organizations that already exist, you also have the opportunity to invent life tomorrow.

Women these days have more education than men in all fields but engineering. They are also the researchers in our society. They're the ones that go online to look for information, and not just for themselves, but for their immediate family and friends as well. And they're the ones who age better because they maintain a social network.

If you ask men after they've retired what they do, chances are they look at the polish on their shoes and they turn to their partners and ask them, "What do we do?" Women are more connected. They want to do more in later life. They are also the number one primary caregivers of an aging society. So women's roles, assumed responsibilities, education, and willingness to use technology for a defined purpose make them a catalyst for change. That's both in the home– as the chief consumer officer of every household in the world– and in the marketplace.

DR. JOSEPH COUGHLIN ON TECHNOLOGY: WEARABLES AS THE NEW HEALTH PLATFORM

Wearables are becoming the new health platform, particularly for chronic conditions and the like. The challenge for the Internet of Things (IoT) and related wearables market is that if they become only the platform for the 'medicalization' of aging, then they will fail. They will be driven only by a market that says, "Can we be reimbursed by public or private insurance?"

These technologies will become part of our lives when they introduce more than medical care in quantified living about how well I feel today. When it's about how well they introduce fun, how well they remind me of places and spaces I've enjoyed, how well they remind me of how to connect with friends and family– so, going well beyond shelter, water, and "Did you take your medications today?"

Unfortunately, the IoT and related wearables right now are being introduced by everything from startups to major Fortune 500 companies that still use the old vision of old age. It's all about "Can I keep you from falling?" and "Can I remind you to take your meds?" But, the companies that will win, the organizations that will deliver innovation, and the people that will benefit are those that create a new vision of what to do with those extra years of life that goes well beyond a medical condition. That takes into account that I may have one or two or three chronic diseases, but I can walk a dog, I can garden, I can work part-time, I can go to school– not just to take classes, but to get a degree because I want to– or I can connect with family and friends.

Wearables, technology and the like are enabling devices. If we don't use them carefully, we'll be relegated to simply taking our blood pressure or glucose level, and making sure we took our meds for the day.

REFERENCES

1. *www.youtube.com/watch?v=0WAdyqxnKBI*

2. *agelab.mit.edu/about-agelab*

3. *agelab.mit.edu/people/joseph-f-coughlin*

Be Prepared

BE A MENTOR

By Dr. Debbie Heiser

I write this as a psychologist with more than twenty years of experience as a researcher and advocate for those 50 and older. So often, I've talked with people who wonder if they've already lived the best years of their lives. Having a career and raising a family take up most of our time between 30 and 60. Once retirement and the empty nest looms, people often wonder, "Is there anything left to look forward to?" This time of life can be emotionally troubling for many. After all, most of us spend decades of our lives trying to achieve personal goals, family goals and work goals. Once we've mastered them, it seems that we are done. But that is wrong! Our lives are just beginning again! There is a new cycle to look forward to.

What many people don't know is that midlife and beyond make up our most meaningful years. All of those years raising kids, developing and maintaining meaningful relationships and honing work skills aren't wasted. A new chapter begins. And it is a meaningful chapter. Midlife is when we begin to understand our life's purpose and we are able to decide what mark we want to leave on the world.

HOW DO WE LEAVE A MARK ON THE WORLD AND BRING MEANING TO OUR LIVES?

By giving back. This may not sound right. It always feels good to get something. How can giving back feel good or be even better than getting? Here's how: by changing lives forever and impacting the world. The knowledge that we are leaving a lasting mark on the world is far more powerful, and gives us the same euphoric feelings we get from the short term, like a new handbag or gift from someone. In fact, it is even better. Giving is longer-lasting. The euphoric feeling is beyond temporary, and actually leads to long-lasting physical and emotional well-being.

WHAT CAN I DO?

Mentor. Mentorship is at least as powerful for the mentor as it is for the mentee. Mentors change lives forever. Their life-long work makes an impact in the world. Many mentors feel a sense of redemption for past wrongdoings, and the most enduring effect of them all, is the legacy they leave. As we near the third chapter of our lives, the effects of mentoring make us feel that our lives were worth living. There is clear evidence that giving back leads to better lives for all of us as we age.

HOW?

By feeling connected to others, feeling valued, and knowing our lives have meaning. Through giving, guiding, and caring for others we are leaving a legacy– a piece of ourselves– that remains in the world after we shed our mortal coil. Each person we train, teach or guide takes a piece of us and passes it on through innovation, interactions with others, behaviors or decisions they make in life. This goes on and on through generations and centuries. As mentors, we become symbolically immortal.

Mentoring is a way to make meaning of all of our accumulated knowledge, skills, values and culture. You can mentor formally, as in your field of work, or informally as a grandparent, coach, or tutor. There are more than 200 million adult Americans who can benefit from the personal gain that comes from giving back to others. It is a relationship and connection with another person. The sooner we learn 'Tis better to give than to receive,' the sooner we can begin reaping the physical and emotional benefits of giving back.

WE ARE BUILT TO GIVE

Developmentally, we are built to give back. Psychologists call this generativity, a term coined by the famed psychologist Erik Erikson. As we pass through midlife, we have a desire to give back, and to care for others without the expectation of anything in return. We get enormous pleasure and satisfaction when we see others succeed, learn and benefit from our guidance. This stage leads us toward wisdom, and leaves us feeling content with life. The opposite of this, for those who don't reach this stage, is despair. We have all met these individuals. They are the ones who never seem to be satisfied, who always feel like they are missing out, or are being cheated somehow. They can't possibly give to someone else because they will feel like they are losing out. A famous example of someone overcoming this despair is Ebenezer Scrooge, the protagonist in Charles Dickens' *A Christmas Carol*, who realizes the benefits of giving and changes his miserly ways and so gains happiness in his later years. The message is the same across major religions since the beginning of recorded time. Giving is good. No matter our age, we can get to the stage of generativity, to give back to others and achieve the blessings of life that come with giving back.

HEALTH BENEFITS OF MENTORSHIP

People who give of themselves have better physical and emotional lives. And it is never too late to start. As Stephen Post and Jill Neimark say in their bestseller *Why Good Things Happen to Good People,* "Giving to others helps us forgive ourselves for our own mistakes, which is key to a sense of well-being."

Research from Harvard's 75-year-long grant study reveals that, to age well, we must have meaningful human connections, which is necessary when mentoring others. In 2015, a Psychological Science article showed that highly generative adults (mentors are in this category) view life in a more positive light than those who are less generative. A Harvard Business Review article from 2016 states "older people who mentor and support younger people in work and in life are three times as likely to be happy as those who fail to engage in this way." No matter when you start the process of giving, the effects are positive. We experience lower stress levels and feelings of redemption, pleasure, fulfillment and happiness.

Regardless of background, race, gender, income, profession or age, we are all similar in how we develop and progress through the lifespan. All of us are built to give back. It doesn't have to cost a penny, yet the rewards are far greater than any monetary reward a person could obtain. Our legacies are based on how we give back to others. We live on long after we physically leave this world through our actions, values, and the culture we pass on to our mentees. Our legacy is the greatest gift we can give to ourselves and to the world.

Be a Mentor

BE CHALLENGED

By Thomas F. Matt

I think SELF-AWARENESS is probably the most IMPORTANT THING toward being a CHAMPION.

Billie Jean King

Opening yourself to new challenges is a key to improving the journey that is life. For way too long, I stayed in the 'lanes' of what I knew: not so much comfortable, but more along the lines of regimented. Some may even say, myself included, the OCD-like mindset puts you into the familiar, and what you know works. I find myself doing this in all different areas of my life: workouts, food, rest, work and lastly, reading. I have to admit– rigidness can become an anchor at times to growth, and it can be the catalyst that is a key driver.

I have never been a 'fiction' reader. In my quest for self-improvement and the 500+ books I have read since 2009, I'd guess that over 90% were non-fiction. Between biographies, fitness, psychology, nutrition, science, medicine, marketing, technology and whatever else I'm forgetting right now, my dance card is pretty full. Why in the heck would I want to waste my valuable time reading made-up stories? How could this possibly assist my knowledge, how could this become an asset? And why would I want to read fantasy novels written for children?

The answer is, I wouldn't, and didn't. That is, until I was recently loaned the first Harry Potter book.

Seriously, Harry Potter!

Ok, so, back story: My family is all about the Potter craze. Now that I have put a tiny amount of effort into it, I'm seeing that Potter Mania is pretty massive. I mean, you would have to be a troll of Potter proportions (pun intended) not to realize that this whole series (Did you know there are seven books and eight movies? Damn!) is pretty immense.

And I must warn you that I may digress even more than normal, because, well, you'll see!

BE CHALLENGED

In our household, Lauren (our youngest daughter) and Sandy (my wife) are true, die-hard Potter-Heads. They have read all of the books and have watched the movies multiple times. We own them all. I had none of it! In a way, I actually kinda felt a little left out. As a man who loves to play the Catholic guilt card, how could they NOT want me in? They couldn't care less.

After years of wandering in the desert that is our house while they were engrossed in the books, just burying themselves, talking amongst themselves, happy as hell when new books/films came out; I sort of relented in my lack of interest. Actually, to be perfectly honest, the guilt trip of 'dad not being invited' wasn't working, and I really needed to know more. I may be stubborn, but hey, I'm not completely ignorant.

I cannot take British dialogue in movies. There is a complete disconnect in my brain when watching films with that dreadful British 'Twang,' so this actually led to my avoidance of the Potter films. Hallelujah for subtitles!

Since the family watched the movies multiple times, I would inadvertently stumble into the living room, like the former drunken sailor that I was, and see all of this Potterism stuff. If you come into this from different timelines, films, etc., Potter Mania gets really confusing. It reminded me of my brothers and their obsession with *The Lord of the Rings* (which, frankly, soured me on the Potter stuff, because that addiction is crazier than Potterism!) So, you could see, my rigid '50s-style brain was having a tough time. I needed a strategy. Ahhhhh, there is this new thing called 'Binge-Watching.' Perfect. I could set this whole thing up with the family as my pseudo-narrators, and with subtitles turned on, I may just be able to get into this Potterness. The plan was to start from the first film, *Harry Potter and the Sorcerer's Stone,* and work my way through all of them. So that is what we did. I drove Sandy and Lauren nuts, because I was pausing the film and asking questions about everything. It was kinda brutal for them. Of course, being a world-revolves-around-me guy, what do I care?

After binging on the films, getting the drift, and being the totally super cool dad, I attended two of the premier midnight showings of the last two films with the youngest super-fan, Lauren. I'm the guy that wakes up at 4:30, and yet I did TWO midnight crazy-ass Potter movie premiers. I have to admit at the first one I drank 2 five-hour energy drinks (hate that stuff, don't drink it) and still damn near fell asleep. What can I say? But, that last film, now that was greatness– I stayed awake the whole time.

BE CHALLENGED (AND DRAG YOUR LOVED ONES WITH YOU)

In the first book, there is a key character named Hermione Granger. (Yes, I will get to that part of this story in a second: the actual reading of the book, not just films. My pal Samantha convinced me to read the book is the gist of this whole thing. Just hang on, will ya? It's Potterness!)

J.K. Rowling (Man, I would love to interview her on the radio program) has this awesome way of describing just about everything, and her character development is totally badass. Hermione is played in the films by Emma Watson, and in the book, she really fits the role almost perfectly. Emma Watson is a doll, even when she is a little shit in the first movie. I mean, she was eleven years old when the franchise started (the first film grossed almost a billion dollars, talk about humungous!) and my friend Samantha really does kinda remind me of Hermione. All brainy and know-it-all-ish (nothing personal Sammy). Yes, yes I am getting to the book thing, hang on! Just know that Hermione is a key, and a very well-written, great character. Samantha is, in reality, Hermione!

BE CHALLENGED

Ok, so, flash forward to just last week, my MSU-student pal Samantha and the actual reading of the first book. First, a little back story on this person (yes, me and my never-ending narrative). Samantha can tell you all about my narratives, having been on the receiving end of numerous emails. I think of my emails as 'coaching input,' but I think she considers them a pain in her ass! My early-morning routine at the gym is pretty consistent. Samantha shows up, which she said she would, but I tried to encourage her not to due to her situation working late. But, you can forget telling Hermione (Sam) anything once she has made up her mind. She is a stubborn girl. She came to bring me a copy of the book. Please let me set this up clearly: It was not just her showing up, bleary-eyed and exhausted, looking a little pissed because she could not find her $150 bluetooth gym headset. No, it was her complete enthrallment of helping me, encouraging me, prompting me, and demanding (that may be a tad much, catch the deal here) how virtually important it was for me to read this book. Damn girl, I get it!

I will tell you though, and as I work on the *Generation Us* theme, if we do not try to communicate with our young people, then we have no one to blame but ourselves if the 'generation gap' grows wider. I love my young friends so much, they speak their minds and 'help a brotha out' as I like to say.

Samantha (or is it Hermione?) has her favorite character, some guy named 'Neville Longbottom,' (of course I have absolutely no idea who, what, etc.) described as a "mostly shy, clumsy, introverted boy who was constantly being told by his grandmother that he was not good enough or living up to his parents' accomplishments." I cannot help but like the theme in the books of the underdog overcoming and accomplishing something positive. In the *Sorcerer's Stone,* it would be the last chapter in which this quote made me tear up: (and truthfully there were others; chapter 10 was a fave)

Dumbledore raised his hand. The room gradually fell silent. "There are all kinds of courage," said Dumbledore, smiling. (Dumbledore, for the few living under the rock like me, is the Headmaster of the school the characters attend: Hogwarts School of Witchcraft and Wizardry. He's the man!) *"It takes a great deal of bravery to stand up to our enemies, but just as much to stand up to our friends. I therefore award ten points to Mr. Neville Longbottom."*

This was a key point at the very end of the *Sorcerer's Stone,* and it was so badass!

Generation Us is about outreach in both directions for people!

Jumping to the head of books I am currently reading happens, but a kid's book? Fiction? Fantasy? You've gotta be kidding me. But, I did, and I started this book just like I would all of my others: writing down points and setting up questions. (Talk radio hosts who want to improve, well...)

Amazingly, something really profound began to occur. I fell in love with the J.K. Rowling narrative. And to even make it more impressive, I did a little bit of due diligence and soon realized that she (Rowling) has a completely amazing personal history and story. I did know a little about her, I mean who in the hell does not? Even an under-the-rock, living troll like me knows something about J.K. Rowling. Now it really is crush time, and I blow this book up like a stick of dynamite. Crazy!

BE CHALLENGED

Reading Harry Potter has showed me a brand new way of perceiving literature. As a self-proclaimed 'talker who writes,' this book and the series (because, yes– I am looking at book two, *Harry Potter and the Chamber of Secrets,* and I will start it soon enough) being open to being challenged is good. Opening my mind, not being so myopic, listening and seeing passion from a young woman I admire named Samantha has helped me tremendously. This is the key to our generational success and future. J.K. Rowling is amazing, and so are her books. Take it from a former non-Potter-Head: growth comes anytime you allow your mind to accept change. I have dedicated this chapter to the new Potter-Head I have become.

Oh, and of course, I could not complete this chapter without telling you my favorite character. Actually, since I am still really green at the whole journey, it's a tough call. It could be Hagrid, for his goofiness and loyalty; it certainly could be Professor Albus Dumbledore, smart and always helping the kids; but for me, it has to be Harry Potter himself. An orphaned boy, who for eleven years lived under the stairs of his aunt and uncle's house (who are, really, the biggest turds in the punchbowl), completely unaware of his future greatness. Harry ended up leading a rag-tag bunch of underdogs to a place where everyone wants to be: happiness!

Thanks to my young friend Samantha Medved for being a cool girl, for building her own story of greatness, encouragement and growth. I see now why she loves these books so much.

—–

Be Challenged

BE PROACTIVE

By Debbie Jamieson

The proactive approach to a mistake is to acknowledge it instantly, correct it and learn from it.
Stephen Covey

Are you dreaming of living forever, avoiding the 'normal' signs of aging; like inflammation and pain, joint stiffness and arthritis? Unfortunately, from the moment we are conceived, we are aging. The exciting news is that the fields of science and medicine, including the specialties of nutrition and exercise physiology, continue to expand the wealth of resources we can use to be proactive and slow down the aging process and experience healthy aging.

Even if you are in your youthful twenties or thirties, don't be fooled that signs of aging are years away. In the past decade, the United States has seen an increase in arthritis, heart disease and other diseases in our younger generations. These diseases were once only considered to be part of the senior citizen population. In the U.S., arthritis affects 300,000 children and 53 million adults. Athletic and exercise-related injuries and poor lifestyle choices can all play a role in inflammation, joint damage and other signs of aging.

New developments in science and technology are able to evaluate these early signs of aging, often associated with inflammation in our bodies. The good news is that nutritious foods, daily exercise and other proactive healthy lifestyle choices can reduce inflammation associated with aging.

When I was asked to write a book to share preventive and supportive nutrition and lifestyle strategies for arthritis, it was originally to compliment a pain relief topical spray called EEZ-AWAY which was endorsed by basketball star, Magic Johnson, and sold on an infomercial featuring him with Dr. Tom Jamieson. While researching for the book, reading *Arthritis Relief! Breakthroughs in Natural Healing* (available on Amazon.com and in bookstores), I discovered a wealth of scientific support for natural, drug-free ways to keep joints and ligaments healthier throughout our lifetimes. Recommended by arthritis specialists and holistic practitioners, it has a myriad of tools to help people of all ages keep their joints healthier, repair cartilage and reduce overall inflammation (a contributor of many disease processes and aging).

Here are few important highlights from *Arthritis Relief:*

For many years, health professionals have used the health triangle to illustrate how the body works as a whole and not as a collection of separate parts. There is a functional relationship between the parts and the whole system. This is sometimes referred to as a whole system or systemic approach. For a model to simplify your health goals, visualize and build a health triangle consisting of daily rituals to help healthier aging:

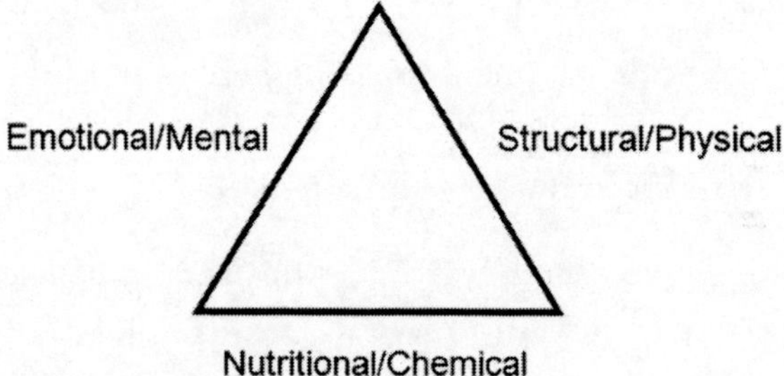

I. NUTRITIONAL

Be nurtured! Balance your blood sugar levels to reduce overall inflammation. Reduce processed foods and added sugars (read labels). Excess sugar drives inflammation. Enjoy daily delicious anti-inflammatory foods such as plant foods (including berries, cherries, apples, and dark green vegetables), quality proteins (such as fatty fish, lentils and beans) and quality fat (such as raw nuts and seeds and extra virgin olive oil). Spice up your foods with turmeric, ginger and other spices (known to help fight inflammation). Make the foundation of your daily eating a diet that is anti-inflammatory! According to Dr. Frank Hu, Harvard School of Public Health Professor of Nutrition and Epidemiology, studies reveal that components (phytonutrients) in whole foods and beverages may have anti-inflammatory effects.

II. MENTAL AND SPIRITUAL

Be joyful, be connected, be growing, be curious and be contributing! Start each day with gratitude and embrace the positive attitudes of continual growth outlined in Tom's Boomers Rock. Be joyful, be connected, be growing, be curious and be contributing every day. Meditate, pray and practice Heart Math techniques– our office recommends the resources at *www.heartmath.com.*

Study participants who scored higher in gratitude levels were associated with better mood, higher quality of sleep, more self-efficacy and less inflammation.

According to research by Paul J. Mills and his colleagues at the University of California/San Diego, biological aging is characterized by a chronic low-grade inflammation level.

III. PHYSICAL

Be active! Be playful! Move and keep moving every day! Staying active can delay and prevent aging. Yoga, Pilates, tai chi, walking, swimming, high intensity interval training and Egoscue exercise techniques are some fun and powerful ways to integrate movement into daily rituals.

—

Based on everything we know, there's no substitute for these exercise programs when it comes to delaying the aging process.
Sreekumaran Nair, M.D., *American Journal of Clinical Nutrition*

—

Be Proactive

BE CURIOUS

By Dr. Deb Feltz

From a very young age, I always wondered about the 'why' and 'how' of things. Why did cats meow, but dogs barked? Why were my sisters built differently than me? Why did people act a certain way? Why was I left-handed, when everyone else in my family was right-handed? Why was I a faster runner than all the boys in my class when I was in the 3rd grade, but by the time I was in the 5th grade, some boys were faster than me?

I always had questions. Being curious led me to searching for answers. Little did I know, as a young girl, that this is what scientists do. I didn't think I could be a scientist. I thought scientists were only men in white lab coats. I had no idea there were social scientists, but that is what I became.

I think the best approach to learning is to be curious–to think of learning as a puzzle to solve. I brought this approach to my teaching. In the courses I have taught in sport and exercise psychology, I've asked my students to write questions that were stimulated from their readings. I called these 'I wonder' questions: they were not questions that could be answered in the textbook, or with a simple yes or no. They had to be head-scratching questions. At first, students had a hard time thinking in this curious way, but they eventually got the hang of it and came up with some really great questions– some could have even been research questions for someone's thesis.

These days, I can look up anything I'm curious about on the internet. I don't have to wait until I can get to the library. For instance, I found that the first known use of the word 'curious' was in the 14th century, marked by desire to investigate and learn. Still, there are many questions for which there are not yet definitive answers. These questions make great puzzles to try and solve.

So, go be curious– about your world, about yourself and about your health.

———

Be Curious

BE HAPPY, BE GRATEFUL

By David G. Hornak

The value of our lives is not determined by what we do for ourselves. The value of our lives is determined by what we do for others.
Simon Sinek

The way someone thinks, acts, reacts and navigates the world can be considered a person's disposition. The world is in need of happy, grateful team players to fill a workforce of skilled employees. Understanding what it means to be happy and grateful is the key to being a team player. Can you picture someone who is always willing to help others? Do you know someone who appears to appreciate everyone and everything they encounter? Do you know people who genuinely wish to work with others? What sets that person apart from others you know and work with on a regular basis? I predict it's their happy and grateful disposition.

In building the case that by being happy and grateful you are more productive, I turn to Matthieu Ricard's quote: *Happiness is a deep sense of flourishing, not a mere pleasurable feeling or fleeting emotion, but an optimal state of being.*[1]

Ricard references a deep sense. Being happy is not necessarily something that a person can turn on or off, but rather, it is a more predictable way of interacting with others. Being grateful tends to impact your state of being, and ultimately impacts your outlook.

As each day passes, leaders are working to build teams of employees to honor and support the missions and visions of organizations. In some cases, employees are rewarded with a financial bonus if a certain target is met. In other cases, an entire team is rewarded if the group is highly productive and meets or exceeds the target. Some organizations are limited by the nature of their industry and are not structured in a way where a financial bonus can be offered. In cases where an organization is not able to motivate by using financial incentives, leaders must seek alternatives to acknowledge the contributions of employees. Without rewarding the positive, organizations are at risk of creating a culture where loyalty is questioned and morale is low. Employees generally feel valued and appreciated when their contributions are acknowledged.

During the period of time when I was writing this chapter, I was fortunate to have had the opportunity to attend a conference with other educational leaders. During a dinner conversation about this project, I mentioned I was writing a piece on what it means to be happy and grateful. The dinner conversation was not only inspiring; it was truly the foundation of how educational leaders from other regions promote a spirit of togetherness by inspiring employees to be happy and grateful.

First, good leaders need to be thoughtful listeners. They need to model the expectations of the organization and work to promote the positive. Leaders of organizations need to ensure the missions and visions are aligned. This alignment ensures that all stakeholders are speaking a common language. By doing so, the foundation of the organization becomes solidified. It is also recommended that leaders recognize happy and grateful team players by acknowledging or highlighting the desired dispositions of those who are thriving in the organization.

Next, when hiring and recruiting new team members, leaders need to be aware on how to identify prospective employees who will serve as team players and have a happy and grateful attitude. Understanding these qualities and personality traits and how to identify them will help strengthen the organization when hiring new employees.

The reality is that we spend much of our life at work. The attitude presented at work impacts the way we handle our challenges each day. According to Tina Hallis, one of the best ways to improve attitude is to model the behavior we value in others. By showing respect, trust, patience and appreciation, the same is likely to be demonstrated in return. Employees generally feel like valuable members of a professional community when contributions are valued and voices are heard. Hallis has generated a list of 12 characteristics that impact a positive work environment and make a difference in the hiring process. The following list contributes to a happy and grateful disposition:

1. Giving positive reinforcement or validating ideas: Send a 'caught being good' note to your employees when you see something you appreciate.

2. Demonstrating gratitude: Thank your employee for something they did, but would not expect to be acknowledged.

3. Spreading happiness: Increase the number of people you greet each day.

4. Motivating others: Place motivating materials in public office spaces.

5. Celebrating wins: Start each meeting with an office or department celebration.

6. Celebrating special events: Remember to acknowledge birthdays.

7. Encouraging positive thinking: Acknowledge and rec-

ognize when a member of your team or office remains positive during a difficult work scenario.

8. Changing the way you respond: Consider an alternative to jumping immediately to defending an idea and begin to validate as often as you can.

9. Get moving: When possible, hold a standing meeting or a walking meeting with your team… and get ready to witness an observable change in disposition!

10. Encourage fun: Add special events to the calendar, such as a favorite team day.

11. Sharing gratitude: Send a postcard to each employee acknowledging special characteristics and how grateful you are to work with them

12. Engage in random acts of kindness: Do something kind for someone else, especially when no one is looking![2]

Hiring happy and grateful people will pay dividends to your organization or team. Hiring an employee with a happy and grateful disposition will leave a legacy. You have a choice, whether you are the employer who seeks a happy and grateful employee, or the prospective employee who has the choice to make the difference. You will be remembered for what you do for others. Attitude is everything, so pick a good one! I hope you choose to be happy and grateful– it is the only way to make it through the day!

REFERENCES

1. *matthieuricard.org/en/books/the-skill-of-happiness*

2. *good.co/blog/create-positive-work-environment/*

Be Happy, Be Grateful

BE POWERFUL, BE PROUD

By Mike Secord

One can have no smaller or greater MASTERY than mastery of oneself. LEONARDO DA VINCI

I wanted to share some of my perspectives through my near-two-year battle with kidney cancer, that has metastasized and moved to my lungs and brain– and how the words powerful and proud have helped to keep me motivated and keep me fighting this disease.

My journey began on Superbowl Sunday– February 7, 2016– at the age of 43. Plans of watching the game with friends changed quickly after I went to our local Redi-Care with what was, by all accounts, a kidney stone. Things continued to change as I was diagnosed with a nearly 5-pound tumor engulfing my right kidney. I was admitted to the hospital, and once the pain was under control, I underwent a right nephrectomy, taking out the kidney and tumor. In the coming weeks I sought a second opinion at The University of Michigan Comprehensive Cancer Center. This is where a powerful first showed up in my journey. It was shift-change time for medical staff at 7am. Being from DeWitt, living in East Lansing, working for Michigan State University and being a lifetime Spartan fan; you could say I was already feeling a little uneasy on enemy grounds in Ann Arbor. We had a little time to waste before my appointment, so we grabbed a seat at a coffee stand located in one of the foot-traffic hallways connecting the cancer center and main hospital for staff and visitors. Almost immediately, my eyes drifted from all the maize & blue to the crowd of nurses turning the corner, headed right at me. Shift-change had arrived and I was instantly pleased to see all of the green & white headgear and beanies! In the midst of all my anxiety and worry, I had forgotten that it was St. Patrick's Day: The one day of the year that some of the best nurses from MSU can proudly show their true colors as they work hand-in-hand with some of the best doctors out there. Very proud and powerful.

My second story also happened very early on in our trips to Ann Arbor. We walked by the financial aid office for patients needing assistance. We saw a young girl, probably 10 or 11, sitting on the bench outside the office. She was obviously going through a battle with cancer, looking weak, scared and wrapped in a blanket & wearing a pullover winter skull cap. It hit me like a ton of bricks that she's going through the fight of her life and her parents are inside the office looking for financial help to continue the battle. It about killed me to think that some people don't have the medical benefits to even give them a fair chance to fight. I have been blessed, even in fighting cancer, that I have been given the luxury of finances and a medical package to try anything available for my treatment and not hesitate because of money or insurance. How the hell do you walk by that and not try and help? I made my mind up, right then and there, to do something. With the help of friends, we began the Secord Strong bracelet-giving campaign, with proceeds going to help others through the Helping Hands funding program at UM Health Systems and to help those going through a battle or treatment at UMCCC. To date, we have raised nearly $15,000 through selling the bracelets and through associated fundraising events. These efforts have made me so proud and have given me a ton of power as I continue my own battle. This world truly is a better place when people simply help people.

One way that cancer has changed me is how I look at and rationalize time. Looking at things 1, 5, 10 or more years at a time, my perspective suddenly shrunk drastically. I began living three months at a time around my routine scans. Every 90 days or so, I get to hear either good and encouraging news, or more terrible news about this horrible disease that is trying to kill me. I started setting short-term goals, like getting strength back, contributing at work, special occasions, etc. Having these goals has helped to keep me motivated and driven. Getting back to work helped me to feel powerful. In addition, I made it to my own wedding in August 2016, less than two months from undergoing inpatient IL-2 treatments that took their toll. Pretty powerful indeed.

My battle isn't over, and cancer will be with me the rest of my days. However, it doesn't have to steer my life. I can control my goals, attitude and perseverance. Setting and reaching what seem like short-term goals is a very powerful ally for me. Being proud of who I am, how I deal, how I handle challenges, how I treat people, what I do to help others as well as how I'm remembered, is a moving force in my life and really shows this 'be powerful, be proud' mantra.

Live Hard, Love Harder, Fight Hardest!

Secord Strong

———

Be Powerful, Be Proud

BE RESPECTFUL

By Samantha Medved

One of the first (of many, as I'd come to find out) projects my friend Tom roped me into was coming up with what he refers to as *Be*-isms. Immediately, my input was that people need to be respectful– I didn't hesitate or even think about it. It didn't seem strange to me, at the time, that one of the things I value most, no matter who I'm interacting with, is respect. To me, being respectful means making sure you aren't making someone uncomfortable in their own environment; it means being kind; and most importantly, it means treating everyone you encounter with the same dignity you'd want to receive from them.

The importance of being respectful initially came to mind because I work in a healthcare facility where, unfortunately, our residents and their guests can get away with treating us however they want. After a string of consecutive days being yelled at across a dining room to get a bag of Cheetos/being expected to do anything my boss doesn't feel like doing/diffusing any conflict with the nursing staff, I was probably just worn down by my job– a comment about respect could've just slipped out. Recently, however, my thoughts about respect have reached beyond just wishing everyone said 'please' and 'thank you.'

I currently live with a family friend who I've known for over a decade. He's always been messy and loud, and has never really cared about how he treated other people. I knew all of these things before I signed a lease with him, so my living situation is partially my own fault, but I thought he'd have more courtesy for someone sharing a living space with him. Boy, was I wrong in assuming that if I lived with roommates, we would each clean up our own messes. Instead, I quickly learned that if I wanted my home clean, I'm the sole person responsible for all that cleaning.

Now, I don't want to just sit here and rag on the guy– but this experience has shaped my initial definition of respect. In the past year, I've been embarrassed about having guests over. I've spent 2 straight days deep-cleaning the apartment before, resulting in a grand total of 8 bags of garbage. I've spent more time in my room than I'd ever wanted or planned to, because everywhere else is loud, gross or both. Needless to say, I'm very uncomfortable in my current environment– and it's all because someone doesn't respect me enough to clean up their own mess.

The next portion of my definition comes from the very same place as the original 'be respectful' comment. I always knew that it was important to be kind to people– it's just common sense. Nobody likes talking to a total jerk. Until recently, I didn't realize how much a simple gesture of kindness could impact someone's day. One of the residents who lives in my assigned building has been facing some difficult times recently. I baked cannoli cupcakes for her because she and I always talk about how we both love baking. I thought giving her something sweet was the least I could do. What I didn't predict was the depth of the bond we'd come to share, born from something as simple as cupcakes. She knew that someone was thinking about her, and it helped foster a new friendship. If it's really this easy, why shouldn't we be kind to everyone we meet?

The third part of my definition also was inspired by work, but it's still that disgruntled employee talking. Let's be honest: it feels shitty when someone talks down to you, orders you around or treats you like you're an idiot. Having to endure it regularly, I've made it a personal goal to never strip someone of their dignity. Everyone deserves dignity. I don't care if they're a cook or a doctor, EVERYONE deserves to be treated with respect. Of course, there are other ways to define what respect is, but so far, these are my big three. I urge everyone to make an effort to go out of their way to be kind and respectful to everyone they meet. After all, it can't hurt you in the slightest– and you just might end up making someone's day with something as small as a cupcake.

———

Be Respectful

AFTERWORD

By Thomas F. Matt

A deep sense of love and belonging is an irreducible need of all people. We are biologically, cognitively, physically and spiritually wired to love, to be loved and to belong. When those needs are not met, we don't function as we were meant to. We break. We fall apart. We numb. We ache. We hurt others. We get sick.

Brene Brown

In the end, we all have just one life. And that life is all about the people and relationships in it. Finding balance is an individual thing, but having good people around and in your life makes it all worthwhile. I love creating teams and connecting people because it gives me a sense of both balance and community. I love good people! All the contributors to this book are good people, and I am blessed to have them all in my life. Turning a dream into a mission takes time. It requires thought, determination, persistence and faith. I believe in what we are doing, so we do what we do.

Belonging to something is crucial to living a positive life, and of that I am certain. We are all fallible, but when we allow our inner voice to spin us into a dark place, regret and failure can rise up and dominate our existence. Through this book and the upcoming ones which will live under the *Generation Us* mantle, I want to drive inspiration and build optimism. This will lead to motivating and energizing positive change, and gives darkness no room to flourish.

The primary paradigm of our journey together is building connectedness. As we connect, we can become engaged in communication. Intergenerational love and togetherness is built on a solid foundation of communication. Culturally speaking, we gain technological connectedness while we lose interpersonal engagement. *Generation Us* is about fostering community, an all-inclusive society of different demographics, ages and beliefs. A value-driven, scalable family– kind of like being part of a giant circus– one I want to get in front of and lead.

Please join us, we need everyone!

Living, Loving, and Learning: Building Benevolent Togetherness; now that is a mouthful– but even more than that, it's a message that came to me in another one of those serendipitous, law-of-attraction moments as we were putting the last touches on this book. I went to the most creative Millennial I know: Miranda Miller. As our graphic designer, she crushes it. As a person who takes my thoughts and helps distill them, she is great. So, when the title resonated with her, that sealed the deal for me. I don't think I've ever used the word 'benevolent' in anything I have written. Frankly, I had to look it up to make sure I had it right. I hope everyone gets it. Well-meaning, compassionate and kindly: yep, that sealed it!

I specifically placed our last two chapters as such to frame up the paradox that is life. I found that Mike Secord's *Be Powerful* submission, detailing his battle with cancer; followed by Samantha Medved's *Be Respectful*; supports the theme of our *Raising the BAR* graphic.

Paradox of perspectives: that is what *Generation Us* is all about!

'BE'-ISMS

Samantha Medved was the youngest contributor to the book, and is one of the four original students who assisted me with the *Be*-ism list and the *Generation Us* speaking engagement. At nineteen, she has good input that adds huge value to the book. Mike Secord illustrates the inevitability of what all of us will have to deal with at some point. Everyone wants respect (Samantha) and everyone will deal with mortality (Mike).

TO BE POWERFUL AND TO BE RESPECTFUL IS A PARADOX

As I shared in the opening of the book, the *Be*-ism list came to me in various states of mind and time. There are certainly many more words that can (and I hope will) be added, but in the beginning, I had personally written 97 *Be*-isms, with my student friends coming up with another 22:

Be interested, be mindful, be accepting, be willing (to listen, learn, understand), be open, be humble, be compassionate, be considerate, be perceptive, be calm, be patient, be hungry, be proud, be ready, be powerful, be yourself, be patient, be loving, be encouraging, be respectful, be courageous, be you.

Young people– wow, they are special!

This list really got me thinking, creating and crystallizing what we needed to do. When we *Raise the BAR* we *Believe,*

Accept, Respect all, we walk the walk, we talk the talk, we do all we can do. Respecting a person– no matter how old, what sex, sexual orientation, religion– is important. To 'be you' means what to a college student? To 'be you' to a nonagenarian (someone between 90 & 100) is something different (or is it?) This is the *Generation Us* paradigm of the 21st century, and it is a beautiful thing. Find a parade and get in front of it. Our tribe is growing, our mission is clear; this is a lifestyle that encompasses many values and desires. To change culture, we have to work together. Nothing is accomplished alone. Nothing valuable is achieved easily.

Let us all 'be respectful,' 'be kind,' 'be accepting' and 'be believers.'

Together we all can make a difference by just raising each of our own personal *BARs*.

'Be challenged,' 'be compassionate' and 'be engaged' in the process that is *Generation Us*.

CLOSING

This book is only the first of many in a series under the *Generation Us* mantle! I need and want everyone who reads this to understand that it is all about 'Us,' because there is no I in 'Us.'

The efforts of all of our contributors to this anthology are duly noted and sincerely appreciated. I would be remiss if I did not mention some key contributors:

First, I thank the 'Fabulous Four' young people who met with me about this project long before the book was ever conceived. To Karri Shalosky, Matthew Elleweke, Samantha Medved and Colin Jackson; I give my sincerest thanks and deepest well-wishes. It was through these four that the *Be*-ism list took root and grew. It was only after I met with these fantastically-educated young people (and saw their suggested *Be*-isms that I hadn't thought of) that I realized how important it is to collaborate with our young people. I can't emphasize enough how critical it is to ask for and value their input– every generation has ambitions and dreams. To these four, I say: I love you, and thank you so much for helping with this project.

To all of the contributors of the book: Dr. Debbie Heiser, Colin Milner, Sky Bergman, Lisa Cini, Dr. David Hornak, Dr. Deb Feltz, Samantha Medved, Colin Jackson, Brandon Townsend, Debbie Jamieson, Nick Tijerina, and Bill Kost; Thank you for your efforts and for believing in this project. Love all of you!

A special thanks to Mike Secord and his wife Liza for doing what you have to do in the journey through your illness. I am so thankful to call you both my friends, and my heart burns deeply for your continual battle. Secord Strong, baby! Love you two, keep on keeping on!

To Kerry Hannon, for doing all she does, and for contributing the foreword to this book. Her agreement to write the foreword so early on validated, in my mind, the power of what we're doing– that it's good and it's needed. Thank you, Kerry, for being my friend and my colleague in radio and in writing. Love you!

To Mickey Hadick and Craig Stiles: two warriors, who believe not only in our work, but in my personal efforts. You both inspire me to continue to 'work it' and 'stay the course.' Overnight success comes to some people ten years in, and when it does, it's fabulous. Love both of you men so much!

To our testimonial writers– Vennie Gore, my gym buddy and mentor; Miranda Miller (*mirandamakesthings.com)*, our beautiful and talented graphic designer; Wendi Burkhardt, CEO of *Silvernest*, a great radio guest and person; Katie Lynwood, a supreme elder law attorney of *Buhl, Little, Lynwood and Harris PLC* and also friend, radio guest and expert; and Chris Johnson, my bud, and also an inspiring mentor, CEO of *On Target Living;* thank you.

And to Jo-Anne Lema from *After Fifty Living*, a radio expert guest and significant friend, you are a wonderful lady, and I am so happy we reconnected. I look forward to our collaboration and affiliation.

To my colleagues at MSU Telecom Systems, all of you

who support our effort– Doug Resseguie, Chuck Harden, Scott Markham, Adam Joyce, Bob Cupp, Jason Munschy, AJ McCoy, Chris Grewe, David Patton, Drew Morris, Nick Kwiatkowski and Mitch "Tree Trunk" Gast. Thank you guys, for putting up with me, and for being my friends.

To my daughters, Ashley and Lauren: two wonderful people who I love so much. Thank you for being my daughters, and for being good people.

To all of my siblings– Jim, Bill, George and my wonderful sister Karen; to Dana, Gordy, Renee and Rochelle: all of you are greatness in my book! Loving you is not nearly enough, but has to be said somehow. You guys are so solid!

To my radio guests, who make our programming awesome, thank you all. To my producer Ezra Bakker, the man behind the voice, thank you bro. To David Demarco, Nick Chase, Chris Tyler & Shelley Forell; the crew at TownSquare Media, thank you all. To all of the stations that carry our show; to Will Tieman and his beautiful wife Wendy, two people who kept telling me to 'stick with it,' thank you. To MSU's WKAR, Peter Whorf and Susie Elkins, it's humbling to be on your air. Thank you.

Special and heartfelt thanks, again, to Miranda Miller. I mention Miranda twice because she has been so helpful, and has taught me the ins and outs of creative collaboration. Her making graphic magic out of my crazy 'brain dumps' is exciting and fuels *Generation Us*. I owe you so much and love how you've grown and become such a talented professional. I knew the first time I met you that you were special, and you have never stopped amazing me with your talents. Working with this Millennial has taught me so much. She makes us look good! Sandy & I love you so much!

And lastly, to my beautiful wife Sandy– who tolerates my crazy behavior, encourages our growth, allows me to buy books by the truckload and keeps our family and business in line. Without her behind-the-scenes work, none of this would happen. She is a gift and I am blessed to have her in my life. Thank you, Blondie, love you, and let's keep this ship flying!

THOMAS F. MATT, BOOMER
Founder, *Boomers Rock*
Tom@*BoomersRock.us*
